Reaching for the STARs

Part 2
Effective Programs and Strategies for Working with Students At-Risk

Dedication: This book is dedicated to anyone who has caught a falling star and given it a place to shine.

Reaching for the STARs

A Resource Book
Published by the Educational Services Committee
OSSTF, 2001

Authors
>   Angie Dornai
>   >   Middlefield Collegiate Institute, Markham
>   >   York Region District School Board
>   >   District 16

>   Jennifer Johnson
>   >   Alexander Mackenzie High School, Richmond Hill
>   >   York Region District School Board
>   >   District 16

>   Penny Smith
>   >   Peel District School Board
>   >   District 19

>   Vickie L. Thomas
>   >   Western Secondary School
>   >   Greater Essex School Board
>   >   District 9

Editor and Director - Resource Books
>   Larry Chud
>   >   District 20

Cover Design
>   David Sheridan
>   >   Thousand Island Secondary School
>   >   Upper Canada District School Board
>   >   District 27

Desktop Publishing
>   Sandra Smith
>   >   Aldershot High School
>   >   District 20

ISBN #0-920930-79-4
OSSTF©2001
Ontario Secondary School Teachers' Federation
60 Mobile Drive, Toronto, Ontario   M4A 2P3

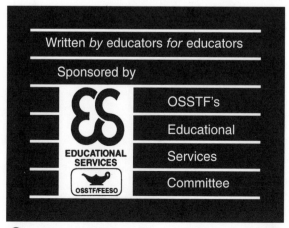

Written *by* educators *for* educators

Sponsored by

EDUCATIONAL SERVICES — OSSTF/FEESO

OSSTF's Educational Services Committee

How to use this book

This book is a resource for information and problem-solving models for students at-risk. It will provide specific information, guidelines and resources for working effectively with students and their parent(s)/guardian(s), and community resources and supports. You don't have to read it from cover to cover. This book is organized by sections to help you quickly locate the information you need.

This book will help clarify concerns about students and create a plan by:

★ Confirming beliefs and observations and thereby enabling schools to identify students at-risk
★ Organizing responses and helping to find what is needed for a particular student or group of students
★ Clarifying roles in the plan and helping to determine other stakeholders' responsibilities
★ Obtaining the supports or resources needed (i.e., who to ask and how to ask for it)

Please note that this resource book has been divided into two parts. Part 1 deals primarily with some of the general issues surrounding students at risk (or STARs, as we like to call them). Part 2 provides more specific classroom strategies. The two parts are meant to be used together as a comprehensive whole. As a result, you will find references to sections of Parts 1 and 2 in both books.

Chapter 1   Alternative Programs

Coping With the New Curriculum, OSSTF's 1999 Resource Guide, states "Some students will have difficulty achieving curriculum expectations and will be at risk of not completing their diploma requirements. Boards are therefore expected to provide a range of programs to assist students in meeting these needs. These programs should include early identification of learning needs, appropriate teaching strategies, ongoing assessment, and communication with parents and students." (33) The Guide goes on to state that 'school boards must ensure that schools develop and implement a range of programs and services for 'at-risk' students.

STAR status - Student of: divorce, drugs, criminal activity. Was tested for a Learning Disability but frequent school changes resulted in no follow-up.

Dear teacher:

I'm a 17 year-old guy who has never school seriously in my life. Back in grade's one to four I tended to always a few grades behind in my reading. Once I hit grade six, I started to smoke cigarettes and drugs. I totally slacked during the sixth grade, but they passed me still.

Throughout Grade seven I turned myself, and others into a bunch of little punks. We were grade sevens smoking cigarettes, drugs and even drinking. That year I failed. Failing was the worst thiing that could of happened to me, because I lost many of my good friend's when they moved on to X, the local high school, and left me behind in grade eight.

My first year in high school was a disaster. My high school was filled with many rich kids who would purchase weed everyday and smoke it with us. Soon many of my friends were chopping weed to make some easy dollars off the rich kids. Towards the end of the year (as the weather got nice) I found myself skipping a lot and getting and sometimes drinking during the school day in the beautiful weather. At the end of June, I was told that there was no way I could pass the year, or go to a ghetto school and receive all my eight credits. So, I chose to go to a ghetto school. That summer many kids from the ghetto area came down to the nice classy area where I used to go to school, and turned the area and many good people corrupt, myself too. Car's were being stolen, housees robbed, people were getting robbed in the parks and lots of drugs were being sold.

The next year at the ghetto school, things turned from bad to worst. I was skipping school daily to get high (I even skipped the first day), getting in

---

fights, causing ruckus and to top it off, lots of the people I meet at and around the schools held heat (guns).

When I was young, I loved being a thug, I mean I look very young and I'm small but people gave me respect because of the people I knew, so size or look doesn't matter. As soon as I turned seven – teen, my thought changed about thugg'n, I started to realize that raising ruckus was dishonest and pointless. I felt sorry for the people we robbed and hurt. I really felt sorry for so many of my good friends that were all corrupt and going nowhere (especially the girls). I had to leave I told myself I had to make something out of my life. Luckily my dad lived in X, which gave me the perfect opportunity to change my ways.

In Sept of 99 I started X high school, I was doing prettygood, I went to class everyday, I had a part time job as a cook, and even got my licence. Half way though the school year at X, some of my friends from Scarborough came down to start a fight. As a result of that I was interrogated by the police and the vice principals. I never told the police or the VP's that I knew the guys, but I guess they knew I was lying because less than a week after the incident the administers at X told me that I didn't have a chance to pass (my grades were 45% average halfway through the year) and that I had bad attendance (four skips), of course the real reason is that they though I was trouble because I came from a ghetto school. From X they sent me to Y's Alt Ed program where I met an amazing teacher named Z, who helped me learn about my learning disability. The program and the teachers were really interested in helping my find my strengths.

Definition

These days much of what is taught in schools encompasses alternative learning and teaching. Schools can really be considered more as asset buildings where a child is prepared to become a fully functioning, contributing member of a complex, multicultural society. The new curriculum emphasizes academic standards and achievement, but teachers must incorporate the teaching and practice of proper manners, appropriate behaviour, socialization, hygiene, respect for others and the environment, and study habits while delivering the expected curriculum.

In the new Ontario Secondary School curriculum, 'Alternative' means a class or program that is different from mainstream school. All alternative programs offer the possibility of credit accumulation, although usually the understanding is that students will acquire credits at their own pace and with greater teacher support. Some alternative programs include a work experience component such as co-op.

Teachers with vision have created alternative programs to meet the needs of a wide range of learners. These programs are offered within the school or off site (store fronts, malls, service clubs, churches arenas, anywhere there is acceptable and accessible space). Administrators should be encouraged to consult with the teacher's in establishing mix of students, location of classroom, and appropriate start, stop and break times.

Some students at risk do much better in an alternative setting. They get more individual academic support and benefit from a more casual classroom atmosphere. They are away from the 'mainstream' pressure to live up to certain reputations. Nor do they have to maintain a constant defence strategy to protect themselves from harassment. Once in the classroom alternative education students often form a bond that provides them with support, confidence and ability to use skills, experiences and values they kept hidden from less supportive peers.

"I believe if somebody would have taken the time to take notice... they could have steered me on a course completely different than the road of destruction that I took." Karla Fay Tucker, first woman executed in Texas since the Civil War.

For students with distractibility issues, it's easier to focus in a smaller class because there is less noise and movement. It is also easier for restless students to take breaks in a small class without disturbing others. Fewer students to disturb mean it is easier for individual students to take breaks when they need to. In small classes where students work independently with individual teacher support, students can move from subject to subject, which can help maximize their ability to focus and sustain productivity. Alternative classrooms provide a supportive atmosphere where students can reclaim their abilities as learners, and experience success.

Purpose

Alternative programs offer an environment that assists students in making academic and social progress by offering an individual pace and expectations. Alternative programs are set up to acknowledge areas of strength and increase comfort in identifying areas in which students need help.

STAR status – E.S.L., negative peer group influence, no parental involvement, Drug use, criminal charges pending.

Dear Teacher:

......so I will be in one of your classes next year. I am just a easy guy to go with but I relly like to joke with my friends, and talk something funny, but don't worry, I respect teacher a lot, no matter who is teaching me, I think wewill having a good time together ...... My background is from _____ about 5 years ago, and I live with my brother, and I have some pretty girlfriends. I realy like to watching movie and going out at night ttime with my friend, but I hope you understand I am not a bad student, but sometime I would never do my homework for some reason, that was just once a while. O.K. I am going to take this straight up, I like Alt Ed. Before, I didn't do good in the mainstream, because I skip too much to going out to having fun, and I hate school too much, I didn't bother to came to school. Also I got arrested before, because I am so stupid to driving a stolen car, but I am finally realize that I should be a good kid, to do good in the school, and never skip classes. Every time I skip because may be I am sleepy, that's why didn't bother to go to class and just skip to go home and sleep. I never skip for doing drugs, I am only doing drugs when I am uin rave. I am always going out at night time that's why I didn't get enough sleep all the time, so that's why I skip at morning class.

Mandated Alternative Programs

All boards must provide a Supervised Alternative to Learning for Excused Pupils (SALEP) program for students age 14 and 15. SALEP is intended for students who are academically unsuccessful even after in-school accommodations have been provided. In some boards SALEP is simply a process to obtain a work permit. In other boards SALEP is a comprehensive program with its own staff, site, academic and work experience components. SALEP is intended as a retention program. The goal is for students to return to full time school after one or two semesters in SALEP.

SALEP is usually managed by a social worker or teacher specifically entrusted with the responsibility for the program. The manager will meet with child and family, complete the required paperwork and track the student's progress while on SALEP. The manager may also chair the SALEP committee meetings and keep the committee informed about the student's progress.

In all boards permission to be in a SALEP program depends on parents' consent. A student cannot receive a SALEP permit unless the principal of the home school receives an application for the SALEP program, signed by the parents. The application must state the reason why the student needs the program and what other accommodations prior to the school prior to considering SALEP has tried. The permit itself is a signed contract between the student, parent and superintendent (representing the board). It specifies the conditions under which the student is allowed to be out of regular full-time school, and provides a time frame for the permit to be in effect. Permits are usually issued for 30 days and then are renewed for a longer period if the student is successful in the program. The student remains on the register of his or her home school while participating in the SALEP program. It is understood that the student will return to his or her home school once the permit has expired. A permit can be rescinded if the student fails to meet the conditions of the permit or if the parent requests the student to attend a regular school program.

Dear teacher:

....I am 18 and my dad runs his own business and my mom also works so they are very busy people. The purpose of me writing this is so that you, the teacher, can eat a slice of the 'real world'. My world. I was born here but my parents come from _____. Until the age of 4 or 5 I grew up in a one-bedroom apartment in _____ Park, a poor neighborhood, where my brothers and me had to leep on mattresses in the living room. My dad was a taxi driver at the time and my mother also worked. Times were hard because we didn't have much money and my parents fought all the time. My father was an alocholic and would yell at my mom no need to say more. When my mom got a job at the bank and my father got a job as a welder we finally moved out. Since then I made a lot of friends but just a feew that I can call good friends. We get together almost everday and just hangout and chill. What do we ddo when we chill? Well, we listen to music, talk and play poop, pick up girls and drugs and sometimes alcohol. That's right, DRUGS! Not bad drugs, just marijuana. I don't know how much you know about drugs and teens but you will see a lot of it going around the years you teach. You will see some students that come to class stoned everyday and their isn't really very much you can do. If you tell the principal they would get suspended and getthem in trouble at home but that wouldn't solve the problem. You need to talk to them and see what's going on in their heads. Remain a cool headed teacher and the students will love you. Some kid's aren't as smartest as the other kids but that's because they need help. You will get some students that will bever dot heir work and instead of saying oh well that's their problem, if they want to succeed they would do their work is not right. If the teacher is unwilling to help the student then mentally the student is discouraged. Instead of giving that student zero all the time, try to find the root of the problem. He might just not want to try in school because he hates it or have big personal and/or family problems that could be interfering. I should know. Everything I've written about here for you has something to do with me but I've tried, with teachers' help, to better myself. You must understand that we are young adults and we are not all perfect – yet.

Perception, Perception, Perception!

As an Alternative Educator, what do you say when people ask you what you teach? Do you say "I work in the Alternative Education Program? Or, in 'Alt Ed?' When you say it fast, does it sound like, I teach the 'all dead' program? Perception is everything. And if we have students who feel like they're a part of the 'all dead' class, then we'll find that we have ourselves a lot of zombies and students who get into trouble at night. From the start, it can be helpful to create a positive name for your program using acronyms, so that there is no negative connotation attached. In addition, the development of a short vision statement, which could be put onto letterhead, can help maintain a positive focus for the program and its participants. Encourage students to get involved in this process too!

Warning: Star Burnout Can Create Black Holes!

Data collected from the Add Health project, a nationwide study of children at-risk, imply that prevention programs fail because they are not based on theory, are not research-based, use one-dimensional strategies, and focus on problem reduction rather than on enhancement of human development. (Positive Peer Solutions)

Sometimes, people make disparaging comments about programs for STARs, about alternative programs and about alternative schools. In some cases, these naysayers are responding to the reality that sometimes alternative classes and programs are merely reactive responses designed to separate the more challenging of our students from those in the mainstream. Similarly, 'alt ed' programs are sometimes staffed not by specially trained educators with qualified support and a quality budget, but rather by the 'odds and ends' of timetable glitches. It is not surprising, then, that the already fragile reputations of our STARS can be further damaged by some close-to-the-mark observations about the lack of integrity in our programs.

Programs should be developed in response to the identified needs of the students. If STARs were able to meet the demands of prescriptive programming, then they would have fared well in the mainstream. Furthermore, teacher education does not acknowledge Alternative Education as an Additional Qualification course. Therefore, it is understandable that these programs become a 'hit or miss' endeavour. Finally, it is a reality that dealing with low budgets, high staff turnover, and little STAR staff support can cause 'star burn out'. Educators who continue on the front lines, servicing STARs' many needs, run the risk of becoming 'black holes'.

The **Checklist on page 9** is designed to help Alternative Educators evaluate how effectively their program is serving STARs. This checklist offers the beginnings of a holistic approach to evaluating alternative programs. It is recommended that this list be revisited periodically for 'continuous improvement' reflection.

> *Catch a falling star and put it in your pocket,*
> *Never let it fade away......*
>
> *Lee Pockniss and Paul Vance, songwriters*

Continuous Improvement Program Assessment for Alternative Programming

Date:_____   Program:_____

1. How does your program incorporate opportunities for:
   a) self reflection for students/staff
   b) personal and academic goal setting for students/staff
   c) periodic assessment of the established goals for students/staff
   d) personal growth for students/staff
   e) networking with regional alternative programs for staff
2. How does your program assess gaps in students' learning?
3. How does your program promote skills acquisition and development?
4. Which skills are being developed in your STAR program, and how often are opportunities deliberately being provided to ensure that the students experience success at those skills? **(See Alternative Education Rubric on page 25.)**
5. How do your students demonstrate recognition of their growth in these areas?
6. What are the indicators by which growth in these areas is measured?
7. How does your program provide opportunities for students to forge links with the community, community leaders and positive role models? (i.e., the police, volunteer agencies, community leaders and/or positive role models?)
8. How does your program set up opportunities for your STARS to shine brightly?
9. How does your program screen out unsuitable candidates so that those who are selected are positioned for success/set up to succeed?
10. Does your program provide the candidates with alternative options within the board so that those who are 'unsuccessful entering your program can have their needs met elsewhere?
11. How does your program make students' personal investments in the program necessary?
12. Does your interview process involve a student background check to make sure that the student is being suitably placed? (i.e., do you "catch" Special Education students whose families have not permitted identification and support, and then, once the student has not been successful, want to come to you?)
13. Does your program have a reputation that makes other students in the school wish that they could be a part of it?
14. Do former STARS still 'drop by' to visit, to touch base, to problem solve, and to chat with some of the newer STARS?
15. Have you checked medical dates with all candidates to eliminate hearing and vision problems as the cause of their difficulty in the mainstream?
16. Have you, with your class, created a vision statement for the program into which everyone buys?
17. Have you taken time for yourself lately, and looked after your own emotional, spiritual, physical and mental well being?
18. Does your program create opportunities to evaluate and respond to your students' emotional, social, physical and psychological needs?

Components of Effective Alternative Programs

(Adapted from Quinn, et.al. *Educational Strategies for Children with Emotional and Behaviour Problems.* Washington, DC: Center for Effective Collaboration and Practice - American Institutes for Research)

Staffing

★ Staff should be qualified, well-trained and have experience working with students with emotional and behaviour problems

★ Chosen teachers should have chosen to teach in these settings. These programs should be staffed appropriately to ensure students are getting appropriate instruction and feel supported by people who want to see them succeed

Assessment of Students

★ Each student should be assessed to find out what they need, both academically and behaviourally

★ The curriculum should be designed around and respond to student needs

★ Assessment and evaluation should not be pre-packaged but be tailored to the needs of each individual child

Practical Curriculum

★ Individualized plans of instruction should be used to meet the vocational, social and life skills of the individual

Instruction

★ Each student's needs (e.g., attention span, interests and learning style) should be taken into consideration

★ A variety of strategies will be used to meet the students' needs

Transition Program

★ A process should be in place to aid the student in transition back into a traditional program or into the workplace

★ This process should begin as soon as the student enters the program, Transition programs should address the skills that each student needs to be successful

Comprehensive Programs

★ Alternative programs should be linked to any community agencies students have been involved with in order to co-ordinate plans to meet the individual needs of students

Support for Students with Disabilities

★ Alternate programs should have small class sizes and intensive instruction
★ Effective and frequent communication among students, families, teachers, social workers, psychologists arid counsellors should be maintained to ensure students receive effective services

A Sample Self-Contained In-School Program

Rationale

MAP (Middlefield's Alternative Education Program) is designed to help students strengthen the skills needed to be academically successful. Academic success in MAP may lead to a return to mainstream education, or, it may be a direct route to OSSD completion, with a view to the student attending College or entering the workforce.

MAP is a program offered to students who:

★ having reached 16 years of age, would realize academic benefits from daily participation in a small group, structured classroom environment with the short-term goals of completing a credit in nine weeks
★ would be able to improve upon attendance and punctuality through close monitoring and a clearly outlined natural consequence structure
★ still require English credits towards their diploma and who would also be interested in completing a Math or Science credit
★ sincerely want to be in MAP and who recognize an inherent opportunity for success conditional upon the fulfillment of attendance and behaviour expectations,
★ who are willing to work towards increased ownership of responsibility, openness to experience, competence, flexible thinking and realistic appraisal of their environment

Operation

* the classes will have a small PTR and will be scheduled in nine week, half day course blocks, allowing for 9 week semester cycles of 2 credits, to promote their academic and personal success
* lessons will be tailored to the needs of the individual but within a larger group context (i.e., the class may cover the same content but the assignments will differ in complexity to meet the academic needs of the individual and the credit earned)
* students are contracted to a maximum of six half day absences per semester, after which they will be demitted from both the program and the school registry for the duration of the semester, and only readmitted upon successful interview with MAP teachers
* curriculum in English, Personal Life Management, Math and Science will be delivered over two nine week semesters, providing students the opportunity to complete four credits in an eighteen week time frame
* behaviour standards in the class to be determined by a) MAP admission expectations (see attached) and b) group policy making as established by MAP students and teachers
* behaviour outside of classroom is subject to terms outlined by school/board Code of Behaviour
* to offset the demands placed upon teacher(s) who work with STARs it is ideal to provide a balanced timetable for them in order to prevent burnout (i.e., assign them an academic course in their subject of interest for the times when they are not teaching alt ed)

Admission/Exiting

Rationale

In order to ensure that MAP successfully meets students' needs, it is essential that only suitable candidates with success potential be admitted. Students who do not demonstrate ongoing commitment to success by way of good attendance and behaviour as outlined in the student contract in MAP will be demitted. At this point, the student may meet with Guidance to explore other options, and may be advised to consider reapplying for the next Alt Ed session after certain mutually agreed upon criteria for the next attempt at admission are established. The student will not be readmitted to mainstream school at this time.

Operation:

★ Students who are attending the program may be referred to MAP by teachers, parents, administration, outside agencies, or through self-election via guidance who will then provide students with **Form A. (see page 24)** This form guides students through the steps by which they can begin the entrance application process. Once guidance has signed the form and indicated which of the available MAP courses the candidate needs then that student must seek MAP teachers' endorsement

★ MAP teachers will endorse suitable candidates after they have been interviewed (usually on videotape) and qualify by a process that may include phone calls to parents/guardians or references and/or through the gathering of information from former schools. These interviews are conducted to determine the suitability of MAP for the student

★ Once the signatures have been obtained from both guidance and alternative education, potential MAP students remain subject to administration's approval. Once qualified, students must return their signed and completed policy forms as their ticket into the program

★ Students who apply from outside of the school must get a Form A signed by administration first. For MAP candidates, the next steps include meeting with alternative educators for an interview and then, if accepted, with guidance to confirm appropriate subject selection. In any case, all new students must complete a new registration form. Please see the **Interview Questionnaire on pages 22-23**. STARs will be disarmingly honest with you if you are direct, straightforward, non-judgemental and honest with them, with a view to helping them understand that your goal is to help them achieve their goals.

★ Students are expected to participate in full day MAP programming. After 18 weeks have been successfully completed, students may petition admin to incorporate aspects of MAP with mainstream programming

★ Students will be demitted from MAP if attendance requirements as outlined in the student policy are not met in either the morning or the afternoon, or if behaviour is deemed unacceptable by the MAP staff or administration.

★ Students will be demitted through the appropriate retirement process in guidance and advised as to appropriate pathways. They will not be permitted to return to the mainstream program at this time; however at semester turn around, they may be reconsidered regular admissions process.

Resources

Operation

Students are strongly encouraged to obtain counselling from an out of service agency to support their success in school. The school may make available Guidance services, and one-to-one counselling once a week with a staff support worker. A Child and Youth Worker and/or a social worker placement student may be with the class one full day per week and may assist staff with academic and behaviour support strategies. These services work best as supplements to outside counselling that can be obtained through calling the central intake information and processing number 1-888-454-6275. It is important to note that wait times for access to services can take up to four months. Therefore, the sooner the process is begun, the sooner the client and/or their families will receive support. Students are further encouraged to proactively enlist support from others, including staff and community mentors, parents or guardians, relatives, employers, self-development programs, probation officers and religious leaders (where applicable) and from peer tutors.

Rationale

Counselling is one of the many processes by which people can examine their lives intelligently. It's a way to have a consultant on solving human problems. It can be good for everyone. It helps people steer, not drift through life.

Students often benefit from an objective reflection of their decision making and can be helped to make important distinctions between feelings versus thoughts. Counsellors help in good decision making processes that can then be applied in practice to the multitude of choices that can be made every day.

Program Delivery

Students will be learning a wide variety of prosocial competencies including decision making skills, empathy awareness, etc., while receiving curriculum delivery in English, Personal Life Management, Math, and Science. Courses run on a nine week cycle of one subject in the morning and one subject in the afternoon. One hundred ten hours per subject will be completed in nine weeks, at which time the second set of subjects will begin. Daily evaluation will include the students' demonstration of realistic goal setting and follow through, commitment to MAP ideals, and student academic performance, evaluated as per course evaluation profiles.

Discipline

Students can expect that for the majority of student/student or student/teacher disagreements, an interview following a conflict resolution model will be conducted and completed, following a suitable cool down period for the parties involved. A cool down time might take place in the hall outside of class, or in the waiting area of the main office.

As outlined under Admissions and Exiting procedures, unacceptable behaviour that is repeated or refractory will result in students leaving the program, and the school, until they reapply at semester turnaround for re-admission to MAP. Students who are demitted will do so through the retirement process in Guidance.

Rationale

The predictability of knowing how conflicts will be resolved often enables those involved to approach the process with insight and a growing degree of confidence in mutually acceptable resolutions. This routine can transfer into the internalization of the conflict resolution process which is one of the prosocial competency goals of the MAP program. Further, the I ESCAPE conflict resolution model reflects preventive classroom management as outlined on pages 10 and 11 of the 1986 Ministry of Ed Behaviour Resource Guide.

Alternative Education Attendance Policy

Students are expected to arrive for class on time each day. Due to the intensive nature of the program and the amount of work covered during a daily class, students who are not present place themselves at a serious disadvantage and jeopardize their chance for success. It is expected that students in this program act in the same manner that they would do in the same manner that they would do in a job situation.

Students are encouraged, whenever possible, to schedule doctor's appointments, job interviews, legal meetings, driver's tests etc. AFTER SCHOOL HOURS, because these absences will contribute to the maximum number of allowable absences for participation in this program. Should a student be unable to make such arrangements, and the teachers accept the note and the student's justification (unavoidable court or doctor's appointments only), the absences may be marked as an excused absence. In order for the absence to be counted as an excused absence, THE FOLLOWING STEPS MUST BE FOLLOWED!

1. The student must notify the morning/afternoon teachers, ahead of time, preferably in person the before the absence, or in **emergency situations,** by phone **before 8:30 am** on the day of absences at _____.

2. The student **must bring** some form of documentation (doctor's note, court document, . . . etc.) and show it to the teacher immediately upon return from the absence. Should either of these steps not be taken, the absence will count as a NON-EXCUSED absence.

Absences

After three non-excused absences (total of both morning/afternoon courses) the student will have to meet with the two teachers to discuss his/her attendance. At this time, the teacher will put the MAP student on contract that by way of "one last chance", any further three absences (non-excused) will result in the teachers' recommendation that the student be demitted from MAP at that time. Being demitted from Alt. Ed. means that the student won't have the option of attending school for the remainder of the semester.

After a total of six absences have been accumulated through late time or days away, the student will have to leave the MAP program, as the student will have broken the agreement that entitled him/her to participate in MAP in the first place. Further, students must be in class for 120 hours; more than six half days away will make that requirement impossible to meet. Because the regular school year will have been well under way after six absences, the administration will not re-enter the MAP student into mainstream programming. However the student can reapply to MAP for the second nine-week session.

Lates

In order to assist students with developing punctuality skills, late time will be recorded in 5-minute increments (i.e. 3 minutes will equal 5 min., 7 min. will equal to 10 min.). If a total of 30 minutes of late time is accumulated, one non-excused absence will be recorded, contributing to the maximum six before the student is demitted form the course. While the MAP math of addition is not accurate here, the message is clear, that chronic lates are detrimental to learning, and therefore carry a heavy penalty. Students who are late from earned breaks or negotiated washroom time also accrue late time in this fashion.

Clarification

Absences are accumulated through:

a) lates of half hour totals - every 30 accumulated minutes of 5 minute increments = 1 absence

b) through morning absences, which count as 1 full absence

c) through afternoon absences, which count as 1 full absence

Consequently, one full day's traditional absence equals two absences of the student's permitted six, and if the student arrives 35 minutes late in the morning or afternoon, a day's absence will be entered for that student.

Participation

When students are given homework assignments, it is expected that they will be completed before the next day. If there is a pattern of the student not completing the homework, then the student will be sent home and an absence (1/2-day) will be recorded. After the first homework related absence the student will be sent home directly for each successive time that homework is not done. Therefore it is possible to be demitted from this program for not doing homework.

There is also the issue of sleeping in class. If the student is unable to stay awake during class time then they may be asked to leave for that class, and the absence (1/2 day) will be recorded. After the first sleeping related absence the student will be sent home directly for each successive time that the student falls asleep.

Documentation..... the paper trail to the STARS.......

Note to readers: This stringent approach to attendance is made clear to the students upon choosing to enter the program. Any student who really wants the chance to succeed in alternative education must demonstrate how they plan to successfully attend every day. Because nine weeks is a short enough time for students to 'see the light at the end of the tunnel,' good attendance is realistic and attainable. Students are extremely proud of themselves at the successful end of a nine week term. For those who come close to the magic 'six' half days away, teachers can devise bargains with kids. For example, the school program allows 10 minute 'buybacks' of time for one week's perfect attendance. The policy regarding lates and attendance is best internalized by students through the posting of a chart that reflects the attendance and lates of the students. It is helpful for this visual to have 5 minute increment lines within each day box, reflecting for the students that it only takes one half hour late to equal a day. MAP uses two different coloured highlighters to mark a.m. versus p.m. lates and absences, to help the student see a pattern of behaviour, Further, teachers can write the time, date and reason for each late/absence under the highlighted square. Finally, as a paper trail, it is useful to have the student write in your student log, under his/her section, the time, date and reason they were late. This log also serves the purpose for communicating between staff about students good, less good, and 'red flag' behaviours on their own.

Punctuality and Attendance Chart:

Instructions for using the chart:

★ The public posting of a clearly visible chart helps students see how 'close to the line' they are getting.
★ The 'line of no return' serves as a sobering reminder of the consequences of poor punctuality and attendance.
★ Each box of 60 minutes reflects one absence, which can be acquired through one ½ day's unexcused absence, or through 'late minutes'.
★ Each acquisition of 60 minutes also equals one full absence, teaching the students that lateness really carries a penalty.
★ Different coloured highlighters can be used for different courses – a.m. and p.m. – to show students their attendance and lateness patterns. Further, the dates, times and reasons for lates/absences can be recorded through the highlighted parts, for students to review their reasons for the poor attendance.

★ Some incentives can be considered, like throwing a 'pizza party' for the class, perhaps paid for and directly involving administration, if the entire class has a perfect attendance and punctuality week.

★ Students who have had to leave because they 'hit the line of no return', remain as visible reminders of what can happen....

★ If students are really working hard at good punctuality and attendance, and a deal should be considered, teachers can consider allowing students to 'buy back' time. For example, a student who is only one box away from having to leave might be able to negotiate a 'purchase' of ten minutes off of the chart, if s/he demonstrates a week of perfect attendance.

Student	Student	Student	Student		
THE	**LINE**	**OF**	**NO**	**RETURN!**	
60 55 50 45 40 35 30 25 20 15 10 5	60 55 50 45 40 35 30 25 20 15 10 5	60 55 50 45 40 35 30 25 20 15 10 5	60 55 50 45 40 35 30 25 20 15 10 5	60 55 50 45 40 35 30 25 20 15 10 5	**6**
60 55 50 45 40 35 30 25 20 15 10 5	60 55 50 45 40 35 30 25 20 15 10 5	60 55 50 45 40 35 30 25 20 15 10 5	60 55 50 45 40 35 30 25 20 15 10 5	60 55 50 45 40 35 30 25 20 15 10 5	**5**
60 55 50 45 40 35 30 25 20 15 10 5	60 55 50 45 40 35 30 25 20 15 10 5	60 55 50 45 40 35 30 25 20 15 10 5	60 55 50 45 40 35 30 25 20 15 10 5	60 55 50 45 40 35 30 25 20 15 10 5	**4**
60 55 50 45 40 35 30 25 20 15 10 5	60 55 50 45 40 35 30 25 20 15 10 5	60 55 50 45 40 35 30 25 20 15 10 5	60 55 50 45 40 35 30 25 20 15 10 5	60 55 50 45 40 35 30 25 20 15 10 5	**3**
60 55 50 45 40 35 30 25 20 15 10 5	60 55 50 45 40 35 30 25 20 15 10 5	60 55 50 45 40 35 30 25 20 15 10 5	60 55 50 45 40 35 30 25 20 15 10 5	60 55 50 45 40 35 30 25 20 15 10 5	**2**
60 55 50 45 40 35 30 25 20 15 10 5	60 55 50 45 40 35 30 25 20 15 10 5	60 55 50 45 40 35 30 25 20 15 10 5	60 55 50 45 40 35 30 25 20 15 10 5	60 55 50 45 40 35 30 25 20 15 10 5	**1**

Alternate Education Interview Questionnaire

Date: _____

Name: _____

The name you like to go by:_____

Age:_____ Birth date:_____

Who do you live with? _____

Placement in the family:(i.e. middle of one brother who is 21 and a younger sister who is 12)

_____

How often do you take naps? _____

Usual bedtime on week nights? _____   # of hours you sleep: _____

Usual bedtime on weekends? _____   # of hours you sleep: _____

Date of last vision test?_____   Doctor's recommendation? _____

Date of last hearing test? _____   Result? _____

Date of last dentist/doctor's appointments? _____

Medications:_____ For _____

Do you have any medical conditions or life threatening allergies?_____

_____

Did you fail any grade(s) in elementary school? _____

How many schools have you been to? _____

Why did you change schools? _____

What do you usually eat for:
  breakfast _____

  lunch,_____

  dinner _____

  snack _____

Is there anything else you would like to discuss during the interview?

_____

Thank you for your time. The information that you share will help us get to know you and help us in the planning for your future success!

Sample Interview Questions for STAR Program Candidates:

1. What are your best, worst, and favourite subjects?
2. How do you think that the world sees you?
3. What after school activities are you involved in? Do you have any hobbies or a part time job?
4. How many hours per week? For what do you use the money? (Allows you to see priorities, or if their family is being supported through their work.)
5. Who are the adults in the house and what is your relationship to them?
6. With what cultural group do you most closely identify? (Helps you identify which support services might be of use, and establishes a student's cultural allegiance. Further, you may discover that the student feels an allegiance with rave culture, or with Buddhism, or, with counter-culture, etc.)
7. What kinds of consequences are meted out in the family, for what, and by whom?
8. What do you think your favourite teacher ever would say about you?
9. What would your least favourite teacher say?
10. Overall, what has school been like for you?
11. Have you ever been tested for a Learning Disability, ADD or for Special Ed support?
12. What was your best school experience?
13. What was your worst school experience?
14. What do you see as the reason why you have experienced difficulty in school thus far? Or, what role or responsibility do you see yourself having had in your success/lack of success?
15. Are you prepared to embrace the idea that we are on the same team, that the teachers here are here to help you and that we need complete honesty with each other in order for this program to be a success for you?
16. Do you smoke? If yes, how many per day?_____
17. Which drugs/alcohol do you use? (if any)
18. How often?
19. Do you think that drug/alcohol use affects your success in school?
20. Are you prepared to attend drug/alcohol/family/individual confidential counselling sessions if we recommend them for you, as part of your participation in this program?_____

FORM A ADMISSION TO MIDDLEFIELD'S ALTERNATIVE PROGRAM

This FORM Outlines the process by which a student may/may not be admitted to MAP.

EXTERNAL APPLICANT: Name: _____
External candidate must also complete registration form and supply all documents.

Step One: Meet with the admin. to discuss possible admission process.
Admin. Will initial appropriate space below if Step One approval to continue is granted. If MAP program is determined not to be suitable for candidate, admin will refer student to Guidance for counselling about other York Region Alternative Programs.

Step Two: Students arrange an appointment for an interview with Alternative Ed teachers. Once interview is successfully completed, and MAP teachers accept student as potential student, Alt Ed teachers will initial appropriate spot below, and student must make Guidance appointment for final approval. If not recommended, student will be referred to Guidance to explore other York Region Alternative Programs.

Step Three: Guidance conducts a course prerequisite check, and makes recommendation for final acceptance into the program. Guidance then initials form, and fills out course requirements with student.

INTERNAL CANDIDATE: Name: _____

Step One: Teachers or students or parents refer candidate to Guidance, who conduct prerequisite course check, and fill out course requirement section below. Guidance will initial below if MAP courses meet the academic needs of the students.

Step Two: Student brings form to Alt Ed teachers to arrange an interview, which, if student qualifies, is then signed and submitted to admin for final signature.

Step Three: Student form may be signed by admin, after a meeting between admin and student. The meeting may not be requested, in which case admin may give verbal approval to Guidance or Alt Ed teaching staff.

Below are the signatures from Guidance, Alt Ed and Admin, signifying admission acceptance into MAP. Students are aware that forms to parents must be signed and submitted before student can enter the class. Parent form will be provided to the student once this form has been given to Alt Ed teacher

MAP is appropriate for this student.   Student has been counselled to consider other York
                                                        Region alternatives

_____   Guidance   _____

_____   Alt Ed   _____

_____   Admin   _____

FOR GUIDANCE ONLY:

(choice of Law, Political Science or History in a.m. only)
(choice of General English 10, 11, 12, media, PLM 1, 2 or 3 in p.m. only)

a.m. credit _____ (code)   p.m. credit _____ (code)

a.m. credit _____ (code)   p.m. credit _____ (code)

Sample Rubric for Key Components of Alternate Education Programming

ACADEMIC DEVELOPMENT AND STUDY SKILLS — ALTERNATIVE EDUCATION PROGRAM

CATEGORY	LEVEL 1 (50-59%)	LEVEL 2 (60-69%)	LEVEL 3 (70-79%)	LEVEL 4 (80-100%)
Goal setting	-demonstrates limited ability to identify and appropriately select realistic and attainable short term goals for self as reflected through unsuccessful follow through	-demonstrates some ability to identify and appropriately select realistic and attainable short term goals for self as reflected by sporadically successful follow through	-demonstrates good ability to identify and appropriately select realistic and attainable short term goals for self as reflected by successful follow through	-demonstrates a high degree of ability to identify and appropriately select realistic and attainable short term goals for self as reflected by highly successful follow through
Learning Strategies Applications	-demonstrates limited ability to use specific strategies to gather information and generate attainable short term study goals	-demonstrates some ability to use specific strategies to gather information and generate attainable short term study goals	-demonstrates considerable ability to use specific strategies to gather information and generate attainable short term study goals	-demonstrates a high degree of ability to use specific strategies to gather information and generate attainable short term study goals
Awareness of Learning Strategies	-demonstrates limited ability to identify and describe study strategies like chunking, use of mnemonics, SQ3R, highlighting or brainstorming	-demonstrates some ability to identify and describe study strategies like chunking, use of mnemonics, SQ3R, highlighting or brainstorming	-demonstrates considerable ability to identify and describe study strategies like chunking, use of mnemonics, SQ3R, highlighting or brainstorming	-demonstrates a high degree of ability to identify and describe study strategies like chunking, use of mnemonics, SQ3R, highlighting or brainstorming

ALTERNATIVE EDUCATION PROGRAM

PERSONAL AND SOCIAL DEVELOPMENT

CATEGORY	LEVEL 1 (50-59%)	LEVEL 2 (60-69%)	LEVEL 3 (70-79%)	LEVEL 4 (80-100%)
Integrity	-demonstrates an elementary understanding of the importance of being forthright, reflective, honest and sincere	-demonstrates some understanding of the importance of being forthright, reflective, honest and sincere	- demonstrates good understanding of the importance of being forthright, reflective, honest and sincere	-demonstrates a high degree of ability of understanding the importance of being forthright, reflective, honest and sincere
Self Awareness	-demonstrates limited ability to see self as part of a larger community of learners	-demonstrates some ability to view self as part of a larger community of learners	-demonstrates considerable ability to see self as part of a larger community of learners and effect of self on others	-takes a leadership role helping others see themselves as part of a larger community of learners, through helping them see their effects on other people

COMMUNICATION

CATEGORY	LEVEL 1 (50-59%)	LEVEL 2 (60-69%)	LEVEL 3 (70-79%)	LEVEL 4 (80-100%)
Expressive Language	-demonstrates limited ability to use vocabulary and language conventions to read, write, and speak clearly and correctly	-demonstrates some ability to use vocabulary and language conventions to read, write, and speak clearly and correctly	-demonstrates considerable ability to use vocabulary and language conventions to read, write, and speak clearly and correctly	-demonstrates a high degree of ability to use vocabulary and language conventions to read, write, and speak clearly and correctly
Discussion Skills	-demonstrates limited ability to use listening techniques and oral communication skills to participate in large and small group discussions for a variety of purposes	-demonstrates some ability to use listening techniques and oral communication skills to participate in large and small group discussions for a variety of purposes	-demonstrates considerable ability to use listening techniques and oral communication skills to participate in large and small group discussions for a variety of purposes	-demonstrates a high degree of ability to use listening techniques and oral communication skills to participate in large and small group discussions for a variety of purposes

WORK AND EMPLOYABLITY SKILLS

ALTERNATIVE EDUCATION

CATEGORY	LEVEL 1 (50-59%)	LEVEL 2 (60-69%)	LEVEL 3 (70-79%)	LEVEL 4 (80-100%)
Resume Writing	-demonstrates limited ability to select and use different resume structures when applying for different jobs (i.e. different cover letter for each resume)	-demonstrates some ability to select and use different an organizational pattern to cold call, job search and complete application forms	-demonstrates considerable ability to select and use different an organizational pattern to cold call, job search and complete application forms	-demonstrates a high degree of ability to select and use an organizational pattern to cold call, job search and complete application forms
Job searching	-demonstrates limited ability to use an organizational pattern to cold call, job search and complete application forms	-demonstrates some ability to use an organizational pattern to cold call, job search and complete application forms	-demonstrates considerable ability to use an organizational pattern to cold call, job search and complete application forms	-demonstrates a high degree of ability to use an organizational pattern to cold call, job search and complete application forms
Interviewing skills	-demonstrates limited ability to consistently present personal and experiential positives	-demonstrates some ability to consistently present personal and experiential positives	-demonstrates considerable ability to consistently present personal ad experiential positives	-demonstrates a high degree of ability to consistently present personal and experiential positives
Maintaining a job	-demonstrates limited ability to articulate what qualities s/he possesses which would enable them to maitain the job of their choice	-demonstrates some ability to articulate what qualities s/he possesses which would enable them to maintain the job of their their choice	-demonstrates considerable ability to articulate what qualities s/he possesses which would enable them to maintain the job of their choice	-demonstrates a high degree of ability to articulate what qualities s/he possesses which would enable them to maintain the job of their choice

Create your own Rubric:

Further rubrics can be developed on any topics that need reviewing in alternative education, including:

Career paths: demonstrates _____ ability to demonstrate realistic and attainable career goals

Anger management and assertiveness: demonstrates _____ ability to select and use different anger management and assertiveness training options for self-control

Behaviour: demonstrates _____ ability to understand the positive and negative consequences of behaviour; demonstrate _____ ability to make good behavioural decisions based on accurate predictions of outcomes of behaviour; etc.

Anti-racism strategies – demonstrates _____ ability to understand systemic racism, how to deal positively with racism, how to work towards the alleviation of racism

Special needs students teach lessons in life

Learning to care for each other not taught in books

By Leslie Ferenc, York Region Bureau Chief, THE TORONTO STAR, January 22, 2000

They're square pegs that can't be squeezed into round holds, and for some students it means they never fit in at school.

But for two groups of kids at Middlefield Collegiate Institute in Markham, coming to class has taken on a whole new dynamic thanks to an idea developed by students for students.

First, there's teacher Angie Dornai's alternative education class – 14 streetwise and in some cases smart-aleck tough kids who are bright and articulate but for one reason or another don't fit into the traditional mould. Dornai's class is their last chance.

Then there's Celine Lee-Sam's developmentally delayed class – seven students with a wide-range of disabilities from mile attention deficit hyperactive disorder to severe cerebral palsy. This is the first year for the DD class at Middlefield – one of several special education programs offered at the high school. Until recently, these kids weren't part of the mainstream either.

For all the differences, the two groups of students have one thing in common – they face major roadblocks in life.

But that changed when the kids from the alternative education class decided to do something meaningful for the new kids in the developmentally delayed program and came up with an idea that is breaking down the barriers.

"When the DD program started (this fall), my kids saw that no one was doing anything to meet the new students, so they came up with the idea to buy them presents," Dornai said.

"To know what they needed, my kids decided to get to know the new students. They researched all the disabilities, wrote letters to parents, visited (Toronto's) Variety Village (a centre that helps children with special needs including fitness and sports training) and just started spending time with the kids."

To see them in action, it's hard to believe students such as Mark Chan are having problems in school. The 18-year-old Grade 12 student is patiently calming down his friend Philip Ng.

Philip, 14, has cerebral palsy and mild autism and functions at the level of a 6-month-old. He doesn't speak.

"When I first met Philip, I really wanted to communicate with him," said the soft-spoken Chan. "I do that by always talking to him, by playing with him and watching carefully what he does. Sometimes I hold him – he loves to be touched – and I use a special brush to rub on his head. He really loves that!

"And even though Philip can't tell me, I know I'm getting through to him. He smiles and knows I'm his friend."

The program has given Chan much more than he could ever learn from a book.

"We're doing things that are helping to care for others and all the students are learning from each other," he said. "You can't get that from reading a book."

When the idea to work with the developmentally delayed class was first broached, Aaron Ghanthan, 17, admitted he was hesitant.

"I really wasn't up to it. I didn't know how it could work," said the Grade 12 student.

His doubts melted after he began to get to know the students, among them his pal Hadi Hasnat.

The two kibitz in the hallway as they wait to take a gym class. And like most teen boys, they talk about girls, videos, music, and wrestling.

"I really like this guy," said Hadi, 14, who has cerebral palsy and uses a walker. "I always beat him at arm wrestling."

"You win because you cheat," Ghanthan laughed.

Jennifer Grant, 18, also in Grade 12, said working with Lauren Clements, who has cerebral palsy, gives her a sense of accomplishment.

"At first, I didn't think Lauren could understand what I was saying, but she does. I learn from her as much as she learns from me."

The program is so successful that the two Middlefield classes will meet with students at another area high school and demonstrate it.

Deborah Headly, co-ordinator of the Youth at Risk Project, said Middlefield's program is helping two groups of teens flourish.

"This program supports youth leadership whether young people have challenges or not. It gives them an opportunity to be role models."

Middlefield helps hurricane victims

By Caitlin Drake, Correspondent, ERA Banner '99

The Alternative Education students at Middlefield Collegiate Institute took matters into their own hands when they learned of the destruction in the Dominican Republic caused by Hurricane Georges.

The students, under the leadership of their teacher, organized a food and clothing drive to support the storm victims.

"We've got a lot to give, so why not?" Lindsay Russell said.

"They're people, we're people, and they need the help," her classmate Tiffany Douglas added, after special guest Tony Fernandez of the Toronto Blue Jays, a Dominican, appeared at Middlefield Thursday to personally thank the students.

The students collected clothes and canned goods from their peers by using a points incentive program.

For every item each class donated they received a point.

The class which collects the most points by next Friday will win a pizza party – one of the students' many successful ideas, [the teacher] said.

"They've had to learn to work together as a team, bringing their message to a large group of people," she added.

The drive, launched Oct. 22, has already collected about 3000 items.

This class has also sold pizza, put up posters, made speeches and collected donations from corporations such as Sony Electronics.

The drive is the most successful the school has ever seen, Middlefield student president Aleea Khan said. "It's the biggest turnout we've ever had."

Russell showed Fernandez the bags full of donated clothing, pulling out children's clothes, shirts and pajamas.

Fernandez said Dominicans would be grateful.

"Especially in the countryside, it will be most appreciated," he said. "Every little bit helps."

The other organizers of the drive are Fiona Cheung, Helen Choi, Daniel Essue, Haroon Khalid, Darren Khan and Ravinder Samra. Later, Fernandez signed everything from bats to caps as students crowded to get a look at the famous infielder, recently re-signed by the Jays for the 1999 season

Chapter 2   Special Education Programming

Overview

When an IPRC identifies a student as an exceptional pupil, the principal must ensure that an individual education plan (IEP) for that student is developed and maintained. It must be developed with input from parent(s)/guardian(s) and from the student if he or she is 16 years of age or older. An IEP must be developed within 30 days of the placement of an exceptional pupil in a particular program.

IEPs may also be prepared for students with special needs who are receiving special education programs and/or special education services, but who have not been identified as exceptional by an IPRC. Caution should be exercised, however, in labelling students without proper academic and psychological assessment. Without stringent testing procedures in place, schools and boards run the risk of prejudging students' abilities and misinterpreting social and cultural differences as indicators of ability and potential.

Identification of students' learning needs may qualify them for an array of services and supports within a particular board. However, special education students are not necessarily at-risk. A successful outcome for special education students depends on a good education plan and the ongoing commitment of parents, students, teachers and administrators, as well as local, school-based creativity. Please consult other sections of this book when the student is not responding to the resources and services set out in his/her special education program.

The following items are used in Special Education but may apply to and benefit any student who is a potential STAR. For further explanations of Special Education practices, please consult Ministry guidelines on exceptional students.

Accommodations

Accommodations are those changes to instruction and assessment and evaluation practices which do not change the expectations outlined in the curriculum but do eliminate the negative effect of learning differences or disabilities. For example, scribing for a student on a test is an accommodation if the test is evaluating student knowledge and not student writing. Similarly, if a math test is used to find out whether a student understands a theory or steps in a process, then the use of a calculator would be an acceptable accommodation.

When implementing accommodations the teacher should consider:

★ the instructional level (e.g., use of vocabulary, idioms, etc.)
★ the timing (e.g., the time of day, the duration of the session, etc.);
★ the setting (e.g., one-on-one, in a separate room, etc.);
★ the presentation (e.g., orally, with large print, etc.) and;
★ the response mode (e.g., scribing, tape recorder, word processor, etc.) of the activity/assessment.

Accommodations are most effective when incorporated into the instruction process since they force teachers to clarify what it is they teaching (and therefore assessing) as well as the fact that all students benefit. Accommodations can range from reduced quantity of work to extra time to complete tasks to verbal prompting. The context of the strategy is what determines whether or not it is an accommodation or a modification.

Modifications

Modifications are those changes to instruction and assessment and evaluation practices which change the expectations outlined in the curriculum. For example, reducing the amount of reading and writing required may, in some cases, be a modification of course requirements. Often, the same strategy can be used as an accommodation in the instructional process but becomes a modification in the evaluation process. For example, changing the reading level of course materials in the instructional process is an accommodation, whereas changing the reading level of materials on an evaluation (e.g., test/reading passage) is a modification. Similarly, if a math test is being used to assess whether students have mastered basic math operations (i.e., adding, subtracting, multiplying and dividing) then permitting the use of a calculator would be a modification.

The principal has the authority to grant credits where modifications have been made. For example, if a student has a severe language disability, the principal may wave those expectations that require the student to independently edit his/her writing for spelling and grammar, so long as he/she is able to meet the other expectations in the course. Teachers should carefully track modifications made to course expectations so that principals may make an informed decisions. This effort serves to maintain the integrity of the course while meeting the needs of individual students.

Individual Education Plans (IEPs)

Individual Education Plans (IEPs) may be created with students at-risk, even if they are not formally identified as exceptional students (10-15% of the student population). This document may be used to communicate with classroom teachers and provide consistency across classrooms. Furthermore, it is a working document that may be referred to and updated on an ongoing basis as the needs of the student change. Students with an IEP may also have curriculum expectations **modified**; it is at the discretion of the principal to grant credits where modifications have been made.

While Special Education Resource Teachers (SERTs) are still responsible for the creation of an IEP, classroom teachers are ultimately responsible for the implementation of the IEP. Please keep in mind when creating IEPs that all **accommodations and strategies** should be realistic within the context of your school's programs. Ideally, the IEP is created in **collaboration** with the student's teachers. It is a working document that may change with the needs of the student. Some sources of information are: observation, parental input, student input, academic and psychological reports, the **OSR (see Reaching for the STARs Part I)**

The SERT or classroom teacher may want to **highlight the strategies** that apply to the course in question in order to make the IEP more digestible and make it easier to incorporate the IEP. This way, teachers may itemize and categorize the needs of their students and incorporate appropriate strategies into their instruction and planning.

Finally, classroom teachers must remember to fill in the IEP indicator on **report cards** in order that students receive support consistent with their IEP on the Grade Ten Test of Reading and Writing. This process may be easier to manage if students are coded to indicate that they have an IEP on class lists. **See Reaching for the STARs Part I** for details on how to use your school's Student Administration System (SAS) for this purpose.

Transition Plans

Transition Plans will also serve a student at-risk by setting out clear, attainable short and long-term goals for that student's transition through and beyond school. These working documents are designed to help educators help students establish and achieve their individual goals in the areas of post-secondary education, employment, apprenticeship training, home living, and recreation and leisure. Identified students with an IEP who are 14 years or older are required to have a Transition Plan. The **Checklist on page 40** may be useful as a starting point in assessing student needs.

Individual Student Amount (ISA) Claims

Individual Student Amount (ISA) Claims may be completed for students whose need for intensive support demands additional funding beyond the standard Special Education Per Pupil Amount (SEPPA) grant in order to provide additional staffing or equipment. These additional funding claims require that students be identified with exceptionality through the IPRC process.

However, the funding benefits of ISA claims do support all at-risk students in the school in that additional support staff may be granted to the school based on individual claims. Attaching a CYW or EA to a needy class can meet the needs of individuals, small groups or the entire class. Teachers should be aware, however, that while they may have submitted five successful claims, they will rarely be granted staffing on a one-to-one basis. Since boards determine how the funds are distributed, schools and parents will need to advocate for a fair and equitable sharing of resources in their community to meet the needs of the special programs and populations in their school.

Teaching Practices in Special Education

Whether a school employs a highly integrated model of special education with in-class resource support or a withdrawal approach (i.e., resource room), it is important to examine how we instruct students with cognitive exceptionalities.

> *Special education programs often focus on task analyzing and teaching the isolated components of a cognitive process without simultaneously letting the child participate in the whole cognitive enterprise. Although instruction in the mechanics is important, it must go hand-in-hand with opportunities to experience the whole cognitive enterprise. (Englert, 70)*

Whether in an integrated or withdrawal setting, it is ideal that exceptional students be exposed to the problem-solving and inquiry process with teacher support in the form of scaffolding. By formally presenting the thinking processes involved in tasks in a step-by-step manner students are often able to perform the task at hand. Once the student has been exposed to the problem solving/inquiry process in a meaningful context, he/she will eventually internalize the thinking processes involved.

Where students have difficulty with concepts or there are gaps in their learning, instruction should focus on the language of the topic at hand. Introducing the language and then having the students use the language in a meaningful context will help students to construct meaning around the concepts presented.

In particular, students with disabilities often benefit from the presentation of mathematics content using a language approach.

> *Researchers suggest that conversation among peers allows students the opportunity to rehearse the dialogue, self-talk, cognitive actions, and self-regulatory functions of skilled problem-solvers. (Palincsar, 1986; Palincsar & Brown, 1984) As students explain themselves to one another, they begin to use the language that was introduced to them by the teacher, and begin to appropriate strategies and self-talk that were modeled by the teacher and others in the classroom discourse. This*

moves the control of dialogue [and concepts] and strategies
from the teacher to the group, and finally, to the individual.
(Englert, 72)
"Ultimately it is suggested that teachers must present tasks to
students with disabilities that model the real world of problem
solving; involve multiple correct solutions; and guide students
in generating multiple strategies in problem-solving (Heshius,
1991)." (Englert, 70)

STAR profile – from a student with Asperger's Syndrome.

Our schools are about authority and discipline and this is a barrier that every teacher needs to surpass in order for all students to become happy and fulfilled individuals. A caring teacher who makes his/her students feel important will be successful in instilling a sense of self-worth in them which they will carry for the rest of their lives. Teaching is not a job but a public service of the highest order. It is a challenge yet a privilege to come into a young person's life and introduce them to independence, self-respect and self-love. You must never waver from these principles- because you have an obligation.

As a person with Asperger's Syndrome, I am a critical thinker with high intelligence and a strong vocabulary which masks my emotional and social needs. In order for my full potential to be realized, my teacher should be my friend and comrade, who likes and respects me. I don't have many friends and my relationship with my teacher is very important to me. A well-intentioned teacher must be sincere in his/her communication and not be condescending or professional. A teacher must never betray my trust by speaking about private matters behind my back.

The most diffcult period that I encounter in school is the first few weeks. I am very picky about where I sit, which is at the front of the classroom. Teachers should be well informed about my needs before the course begins and have something suitable worked out. It is very embarrassing for my teacher to say "I spoke with your Special Education teacher and am aware of your condition" in class. All arrangements should be done privately. I feel anxious in new situations like that and my temper can flare off at any sign of disrespect. Teachers should be positive and allow concessions. The teacher sends mixed messages when he/she tells the student with Aspergers to not interupt yet allows others to do so in some situations. Such rules should be enforced equally but differently, with ample consideration given for the Asperger's students diffulties. I should receive many "chances" and opportunities to improve on my behaviour. When I am irate and verbally express my anger to the teacher it is best to deal with the matter in question calmly rather than ignoring or berating me. Often my objections are to petty things to the teacher but are important to me. My teacher must not perceive my arguing as a challenge to his/her authority and discipline me. My teacher should recognise I am very specific with language and my vast knowledge compels me to correct the teacher when I feel appropriate.

Finally, the teacher must accept me as a person and not a disability.

When I think about the students who are labelled "at risk" I wonder what exactly that means. Clearly, I think that most students are "at risk." By the very nature of being a young person growing up in an ever-changing world, they are "at risk" of just about anything. Their lives are impacted by their place in society. My message is not that students have no hope of being successful because of their socio-economic place in society, or their cultural heritage, or their sex, I merely intend to preface my statements with a caution. We must note that there are times when a young person is so impacted by their place in society and the events that surround their lives that they are irreparably damaged and no matter what the interventions they are unable to access them.

It is my belief that as educators we must be inclusive. This clearly, is one of the "buzz" words of today and seems to have many meanings. The meaning I choose to have for this word is that we include all of the experiences the child has. We must not forget that the child comes to the teacher with a complete set baggage of life experiences and so do we as adults. Our job is to attempt to change a belief system. The student has arrived in our school with a set of beliefs that has taken his lifetime to develop. We have the job of introducing a new set of beliefs which can be seen by the student as workable. It is important to acknowledge at this point that we too have a lifetime of experiences and beliefs that may not coincide with the students' set.

In the 30 odd years that I have been working with young people I have found that most come with similar profiles. Initially, no matter how they begin their relationship with you, they generally want you to like them. They want to be accepted and cared for. Some come with a hard shell of protection and show it to anyone who dares come near. Others protect themselves by never letting anyone get close enough to see who the real person is; however, allow you to see what they think you want. What becomes difficult for a teacher is dealing with the student who is aggressively wilful, the student who challenges. These challengers are difficult for teachers since they demand the educator to look at themselves and how they deal with situations. The educator must either accept the student's belif system and support it by responding in the manner the student is used to or respond differently.

When I met Jennifer, I realized immediately that she was a "challenger." Her behavioural profile spoke volumes about what she believed were going to be her experience. She did not smile, look me in the eye or speak about herself. Jennifer barely gave me the time of day. She did know that I was the person who was going to allow her to stay in the school of her choice and therefore begrudgingly allowed me to speak to her. I created a timetable and I also set out the parameters of our relationship. In a tone which expressed caring and yet at the same time clarity of expectations I told her what she could expect. I stated what she could expect from me and was specific about my expectations of her.

Tone at this time point was very important because I did not want to say one thing with words and another with my tone of voice. Prejudging a student because of their demeanour can be easily picked up by a young person through tone and facial expressions. When the adult sends out double messages it really doesn't matter what words you use because the young person doesn't hear them. Jennifer listened and didn't really say much of anything. At this point, I knew that gaining her trust would be difficult. She, like a lot of students I have worked with did not see me as a person. Jennifer saw me as an adult who really was not there to help. Her belief system about adults was working well. She did not trust and didn't see any reason to change.

Jennifer agreed to the expectations laid out to her. She did not verbally create any issues while at school yet was not attending her first period class. Jennifer did not seek any assistance from the Special Education Department or Guidance. She just kept skipping her class. Her teacher had spoken to her on a number of occasions to no avail.

When the attendance situation came to my attention, I spoke to Jennifer, who continued to be reluctant to trust that I would act on her behalf. She had, however, started to come into the Special Education areas to use the computers where she could get some assistance with her English. In an unobtrusive manner I slowly began to provide Jennifer with suggestions of how she could get further help. It was my belief that if I had pushed her too hard Jennifer would have shut me out completely. It was necessary to have a low profile since I believed that Jennifer's distrust of adults was her way of protecting herself. She gradually began to talk to me about her work, a very safe subject since it really was not about her. These talks were basically one-sided with me doing the asking and her providing short safe answers. I asked her if she would like to me help her -- what she would like to do with the problem she was having in her first period class. Jennifer was sixteen years old and quite worldly and because of this I needed to include her in any decisions made about her life. She was quite taken aback with this request since her belief system did not include this strategy. She even stated that she expected that she would just fail or get kicked out. When I was able to place her in a class with a teacher she liked and someone of her cultural heritage Jennifer was amazed. This was the beginning of our relationship.

Many experiences later, Jennifer spoke to me about this event. She told me that I was the first person who really showed her that what she wanted was important. Through modelling trust and honesty Jennifer learned that it was safe to allow herself to be seen. She slowly began to change her belief about herself. Jennifer eventually came to me with many of her life problems and permitted me to help her find solutions to them. Her previous experience that had created a hard shell of protection was slowly changing through her new experiences. Jennifer did not pass the course; however, she did graduate and is enrolled in a college program to work with young people who are "at risk."

Terry Copleston

Transition Plan Checklist for Exceptional Students and STARs

Please indicate how the student meets the following criteria using the following criteria:

Good (G) Fair (F) Needs Improvement (NI)

Academic: The student has:

_____ an understanding of his/her academic strengths and needs

_____ up-to-date assessments on file (where needed)

_____ an understanding of the nature of his/her learning

_____ familiarity with effective accommodations and strategies to promote his/her success

_____ self-advocacy skills in the classroom

_____ realistic career goals

_____ good study skills

_____ good test-taking skills

_____ good presentation skills

_____ good oral expression

_____ computer skills

_____ adequate writing/reading skills

_____ organizational skills

_____ questioning skills

_____ the ability to follow instructions

Career: The student has:

_____ an up-to-date AEP

_____ an awareness of the social/academic/physical demands of him/herself

_____ an awareness of the social/academic/physical demands of his/her chosen career

_____ realistic goals for post-secondary education

_____ realistic career goals

_____ areas of interest which relate to the career goals

_____ taken the initiative to investigate the work place/experience of his/her chosen career

_____ taken the initiative to research the work place/demands of his/her chosen career

_____ a back up plan for his/her chosen education and career path

Communication Skills: The student has:

_____ listening skills

_____ the ability to hold a conversation with peers

_____ the ability to hold a conversation with adults

_____ the ability to ask for what he/she needs

_____ the ability to express him/herself clearly

_____ the ability to express him/herself calmly

_____ letter-writing skills

_____ telephone skills and etiquette

_____ e-mail skills and etiquette

Social Skills: The student has:

_____ an understanding of his/her social strengths and needs

_____ the ability to greet people appropriately

_____ an awareness of how others see him/her

_____ an awareness of the messages certain styles of dress and grooming send

_____ a polite manner

_____ can demonstrate a positive and pleasant manner during interviews

_____ a sense of responsibility to others on a team

_____ respect for others

_____ positive peer relationships

_____ the ability to take directions

_____ leadership potential

Recreation/Leisure: The student has:

_____ interests outside of school: _____

_____ a healthy lifestyle

_____ free time for him/herself

_____ hobbies: _____

Community: The student has:

_____ public transportation skills

_____ the ability to shop for him/herself

_____ the ability to handle money responsibly

_____ the ability to make appointments when necessary

_____ the ability to do personal banking

_____ the ability to seek help in an emergency

_____ the ability to access community supports (e.g., student welfare; scholarship funds)

Home: The student has:

_____ the ability to plan and prepare nutritious meals and snacks

_____ the ability to clean his/her own room

_____ the ability to complete household chores (e.g., laundry)

_____ the ability to budget money

Employment: The student has:

_____ a resume

_____ a relevant cover letter

_____ interest in part-time employment

_____ applied for employment

_____ been employed

_____ kept a job

_____ worked his/her way up in the job

Overall Comments/Next Steps:

_____

_____

_____

Chapter 3   School-to-Work Transition Programs

Context

Life skills are those tasks young people should learn in order to be productive as adults. These skills help young people to negotiate their lives in effective ways. Gaps in life skill development are usually evident for STARs. In particular, these gaps inhibit meaningful transition from school to work. Inability to build social relationships or poor communication skills, disruptive family life, academic challenges, negative self-perception, and social isolation are examples of how limited life skills can individually or collectively hinder the student's development.

Purpose

Career education programs are a vital and valuable component in the secondary schools. Under secondary school reform, more emphasis is being placed on connecting the school to the workplace. School-to-work transition programs are designed to meet the needs of those students who will not be earning an OSSD but would like to prepare for a particular field of employment.

Goal

In this type of program, students will acquire the skills and knowledge that they will need to be productive and successful participants in the workforce.

Design of the Program

The program should include:

★ classroom instruction
★ career training

* workplace values
* orientation and exit programs
* exploration activities
* career counselling

Preparation

During Grades nine and ten, students should choose subjects which upon prepare them to gain access to a particular career (e.g., technology courses) and to further their academic skills (e.g., Locally Developed courses).

Curriculum

The curriculum will emphasize the workplace application of all materials. It will stress the importance of employability skills. Transition plans may be a useful framework for establishing individual goals and needs. Curriculum can then be designed to meet the needs of the group. The transition plan will give meaning to what is learned in the classroom and connect it to the outside world.

The program must provide learning opportunities that will change the way students view themselves and how they fit into the world of work. It must empower the student to set realistic and attainable goals and offer the opportunity to experience success with these goals. The teaching of topics such as learning styles (visual, auditory, kinaesthetic) will also help students identify their strengths and create realistic goals.

In general, the focus will be on three areas of learning which include:

* student development
* interpersonal development
* career development

The Model

The following components will contribute to an effective model for a school-to-work transition program:

Using a Team Approach

★ Board promotion of the model
★ Administrative support
★ Learning support intervention
★ Incorporating support services
★ Involving a co-operative education teacher
★ Incorporating mentors (students and community members)

Guidance/Counselling

Collaboration with guidance counsellors will be necessary to meet the individual needs of students.

Small Class Size

A small class size allows for more individualized attention and is an effective strategy   when working with students who are at -risk.

Curriculum

A curriculum that is flexible and incorporates student input will be most effective. Students should feel empowered by the curriculum and see its relevance to their goals.

Learning Opportunities

Incorporate:

★ Self-assessments: journals, portfolios, personal inventories
★ Job shadowing, observation, guest speakers, etc.
★ Co-operative education experiences
★ Self-directed learning: making personal choices whenever possible
★ Volunteer opportunities: community services, extra-curricular, student-council

Employability Skills Profile

The **Profile on page 47,** can be used as a reference when designing School-to-Work Transition programs. The Employability Skills Assessment (ESA) and the Occupational Work Ethic Inventory may be used to assess students' areas of strengths and needs.

See http:www.coe.uga.edu/cgi-bin/cgiwrap/rhill/esa.pl

and   http://www.coe.uga.edu/cgi-bin/cgiwrap/rhill/owei.pl   for   these interactive surveys.

Employability Skills Profile

The Critical Skills Required by the Canadian Workforce

Academic Skills

(i.e., skills that provide the basic foundation for getting, keeping, and progressing in a job and achieving the best results)

Canadian employers need a person who can:

Communicate
* ★ Understand and speak the languages in which business is conducted
* ★ Listen, to understand and learn
* ★ Read, comprehend, and use written materials, including graphs, charts and displays
* ★ Write effectively in the languages in which business is conducted

Think
* ★ Think critically and act logically to evaluate situations, solve problems, and make decisions
* ★ Understand and solve problems involving mathematics and use the results
* ★ Use technology, instruments, tools, and information systems effectively
* ★ Find and apply specialized knowledge from various fields (e.g., skilld trades, technology, physical sciences, arts, and social sciences

Learn
* ★ Continue to learn for life

Personal Management Skills

(i.e., the combination of skills, attitudes, and behaviour required to get, keep, and progress in a job and achieve the best results)

Canadian employers need a person who can demonstrate:

Positive attitudes and behaviour
* ★ Self-esteem and confidence
* ★ Honesty, integrity, and personal ethics
* ★ A positive attitude toward learning, growth, and personal health
* ★ Initiative, energy, and persistence to get the job done

Responsibility
* ★ The ability to set goals and priorities in work and personal life
* ★ The ability to plan and manage time, money, and other resources to achieve goals
* ★ Accountability for actions taken

Adaptability
★ A positive attitude toward change
★ Recognition of and respect for people's diversity and individual differences
★ The ability to identify and suggest new ideas to get the job done - creativity

---

Teamwork Skills

(i.e., the skills needed for working with others, progressing in a job, and achieving the best results)

Canadian employers need a person who can:

Work with others
★ Understand and contribute to the ogranization's goals
★ Understand and work within the culture of the group
★ Plan and make decisions with others and support the outcomes
★ Respect the thoughts and opinions of others in the group
★ Exercise "give and take" to achieve group results
★ Seek a team approach as appropriate
★ Lead when appropriate, mobilizing the group for high performance

Source: Employability Skills Profile: What are Employers Looking For? Corporate Council on Education, a program of the national Business and Education Centre, Conference Board of Canada, 1992.

Work Experience Skills
(an adaptation)

Student needs to:	Teaching Strategies	Assessment Strategies
❑ Develop or increase vocational skills ❑ Demonstrate cooperative behaviour on the job site ❑ Accept directions from authority figures ❑ Exhibit good work ethics ❑ Follow a sequential order when completing a required task ❑ Use public transportation independently ❑ Behave appropriately in the work environment ❑ Develop independence in personal hygiene ❑ Write resume ❑ Complete a job interview independently	❑ Provide opportunities to develop vocational skills (e.g. collating, folding, labelling, sorting, assembling, packaging) ❑ Provide opportunities for in-school work experience (e.g. recycling, shredding paper, filling pop machines, etc.) ❑ Promote an atmosphere of cooperation (e.g. using groups, assembly line format) ❑ Develop a program/strategies to instil good work ethics (videos, kits, e.g. being on time, completing a task, being reliable, being conscientious) ❑ Develop a task analysis program to break the job into small steps ❑ Set up a bus training program ❑ Provide opportunities to role play and/or model appropriate social skills ❑ Set up a hygiene program (e.g. shower, shave, hair care, deodorant, etc.) ❑ Develop a program to encourage independence in writing resumes (e.g. a model resume) ❑ Model questions and answers from a job interview ❑ Incorporate suggestions from employers/agents	❑ Use guided observation ❑ Maintain checklists ❑ Keep anecdotal records ❑ Monitor productivity ❑ Input from community employers/agents

Chapter 4   Literacy Issues

The new curriculum demands that educators impart more knowledge and skills to students at an earlier age and at a faster rate. Furthermore, the Grade Ten Test of Reading and Writing is a high stakes evaluation which measures a prescribed set of functional literacy standards and content. As schools busily try to prepare their students for this evaluation, it is important not to lose focus on what literacy is and how it is acquired. The following section has been prepared to help schools and teachers of every subject understand the issues at hand and develop some short and long-term strategies to promote high literacy standards in their community.

> *"Poverty is the underlying cause of illiteracy. Without any proven will or ability to break the chains of poverty, no government has been able to make significant progress toward universal literacy."*   *(Myths and Realities of Literacy/Illiteracy:, in* <u>*Convergence*</u>*), Vol. XX, #1, 1987*

What is Literacy?

There are many definitions for literacy whether they be functional, cultural, environmental, computer-related, media-related or academic in their orientations. No matter how you look at it, literacy is a cultural activity. It is how we make meaning in our lives as we interact with the many types of texts and contexts around us.

We tend to reduce literacy to reading and writing skills. For our purposes, literacy may be defined as the act of making meaning through print and related mediums. A literate student knows, understands and communicates using the literary elements of these mediums, including language, graphics, images, and layout and design.

Regardless of context, the basic premise behind literacy is that people understand their world through the meaning they make in the context of their own lives. Text and experience interact to create an individual learning experience. This framework highlights the fact that education is a cultural process and that learning takes place in a cultural context.

The new curriculum in Ontario's secondary schools is based on a core set of concepts and skills. Due to its highly knowledge-based, informational nature, this type of curriculum framework may not provide a meaningful learning experience in and of itself. Schools may be faced with individuals or groups of individuals who are not able to readily connect with this highly rigorous and informational curriculum design. Consequently, the Grade Ten Test of Reading and Writing that is based on this curriculum may be of concern to many students.

The Education Quality and Accountability Office (EQAO) is developing and implementing the Grade Ten Test of Reading and Writing and should be referred to for specifics on the content and format of the test. (www.eqao.org)

Factors Affecting Literacy

★ Curriculum design
★ Instructional strategies
★ Socio-cultural background of students
★ Second language factors
★ Exceptionalities (i.e., learning disabilities)

Fundamental Literacy Issues
When we examine some of the basic principles of comprehension, we are able to put literacy issues into very simple terms. The following

framework may be useful to teachers as they try to determine the needs of groups and individuals in the classroom:

★ **Miscomprehension** occurs when the reader/audience does not understand the perspective of the text. This is apparent in the classroom when students do not relate to the particular views behind the content presented. Educators attempt to counter this effect by teaching about audience awareness and author's intent. However, these strategies can only compensate in a limited fashion when the premises of the given content are contradictory to the fundamental beliefs of learners and incompatible with their experiences.

★ **Noncomprehension** occurs when the format or medium of a given text is not congruent with a child's grasp of language. If the syntax and style of the text are out of reach for the student, the student will be inherently limited in their ability to connect with the meaning of a given text.

★ **Incomprehension** occurs when a reader rejects the meanings presented in a given text. This is a daily occurrence in schools as the learner commits an act of self-preservation. This rejection may occur as a result of social and cultural factors, or simply as a result of varied individual experiences

Miscomprehension, noncomprehension and incomprehension may be paralleled by the constructs of **perspective**, **medium**, and **content**, respectively. This parallel provides educators with three clear criteria with which to examine the curriculum and instructional strategies used in their classrooms. The following chart highlights the three elements:

Comprehension Issues

Type of Comprehension	Issue	Example	Curricular Context
Miscomprehension (perspective)	• Reader doesn't understand the perspective	• A child reading a selection from a religious text without background knowledge of the archetypes and values inherent in that text	• we assume that students relate to the perspectives presented • a result of the top-down structure of curriculum
Noncomprehension (medium)	• syntax/style out of reach	• a child from an oral culture reading Shakespeare	• incongruence with child's oral language
Incomprehension (content)	• reader rejects meaning	• a child whose culture fasts reading about the importance of eating every day	• happens everyday in school • the learner commits an act of self-preservation

Socio-Cultural Issues

"That we cannot tell the dancer from the dance" (Yeats)

Literacy is a socio-cultural issue, not an academic one, and if educators are to ultimately raise the literacy levels of the students in their community, they must be willing to examine the context of literacy in students' lives. Bernard Ferdman's guiding questions (Purcell-Gates, 204) acknowledge the fact that the process of becoming literate is mediated by one's cultural identity. These questions may be useful to schools as they gather information about their students' programming needs:

★ How is literacy defined in the individual's group and what is its significance? What behaviours are included in this definition?

★ What significance do particular texts have for the individual's cultural identity?

★ How do the particular pedagogical approach, the texts that are used, the purpose of literacy as communicated by the school, relate to the learner's motives and sense of identity (and more subtly, what messages does a reading and writing curriculum communicate about the value of the learner's culture?)?

★ What relationship does the learner perceive between tasks assigned in school and his or her cultural identity? Must the learner change his or her self-concept in order to do what is asked?

If what is included in the curriculum is what our culture deems important, then the omissions are powerful statements as to which groups do or do not matter in our society. And while the concept of a common curriculum is neat and tidy, all students do not process information in the same way. We must be aware of the perspectives we promote in our classrooms, both explicit (i.e., in the lessons we teach), and implicit (i.e., in the personal perspectives and narratives which infiltrate our teaching styles).

Traditional paradigms do not recognize the need for authenticity in all acts of literacy. In such paradigms, the classroom is very teacher-centred and dictates what information is to be delivered without consideration of its context. James Gee emphasizes the role of experience in what he calls the learner's primary Discourse – "'a series of nested cultural contexts': Unless one acquires literate behaviours, using print and participating with literate others [meaning those who are embedded in the child's life], one cannot go beyond a simple, often incomplete, mastery of the code." (Purcell-Gates, 181-2)

In an effort to make the curriculum more meaningful for different socio-cultural groups, we often end up creating compensatory programs that only run the risk of fragmenting perspectives even further. That is, teaching black history only to blacks will create what Postman calls "private minds." Conversely, teaching African and Asian history to all will aid in the creation of a "public mind". (Postman, 57) "The idea of public education depends absolutely on the existence of shared narratives *and* the exclusion of narratives that lead to alienation and divisiveness...public education does not serve a public. It creates a public." (Postman, 17-8) In order to promote literacy amongst our young people, perspectives of various backgrounds, ages and experiences should be incorporated in the classroom. This will provide more entry points for marginalized students as well as greater understanding of the issues on the part of all students.

Conceptualizing literacy as cultural behaviour facilitates our ability to recognize the different ways in which print is <u>and is not used </u>by families. Unless one acquires literate behaviours, using print and participating with literate others, one cannot go beyond simple mastery or functional literacy. The social and cultural lives of many students do not support this effort but rather exists separately and often compete with it. It is important to remember that print does not exist independent of experience. And, in our classrooms, it is important to remember that teaching and learning reflect different aspects of one act which is transactional in nature; if students are not learning, we are not teaching them effectively.

Recently, the provincially-mandated *Grade Ten Literacy Test* was renamed the *Grade Ten Test of Reading and Writing*. This change implicitly acknowledges the limited scope of this assessment tool and the extent that literacy issues permeate our lives. While the diligent work of educators to prepare students for such a test will likely result in the advancement of those students who border on the edges of the literacy standard which has been set, our success will be limited. Those students who are socially and culturally at-risk in our system will not be engaged until fundamental changes to the design of our curriculum and the methods of our instruction are made. Until we begin to accommodate the learning needs and perspectives of the many groups who make up our society, true literacy will not be able to be attained, or measured.

All that is implicit is a commitment to what is thought valuable. (R.S. Peters, Ethics and Education. Glenview Ill.: Scot, Foresman, 1967)

Exclusion and Access

Without a commitment to a larger "Canadian" culture, many groups in our society remain excluded from what is deemed mainstream or literate culture. It is necessary to acknowledge the legitimacy of oral cultures as well as dialects in our classrooms. In addition, it is important to remember that written language is a completely separate form of communication to oral language. It contains a more varied vocabulary (which may be used to differentiate social situations and levels), a more complex structure and its units are more 'packed' and are ordered differently. Bureaucratic and academic writing is the most impenetrable to 'outsiders'. It follows that the information and messages communicated through written correspondence by schools is often inaccessible to many parents.

It is also important to remember that many parents are not literate in their first language and that promoting literate behaviours in their child may not be a priority at the present time. In fact, many parents are struggling to meet their child's physical needs and do not have the time or energy to meet their child's academic needs. Involving parents in literacy programs and connecting the child with cultural agencies are two ways of fostering a sense of literacy and parent support for children. Being aware of these issues is the first step toward remedying the situation.

How Do We Tend to Respond?

When students are not experiencing success with the standard curriculum, we tend to provide more intensive instruction in the same irrelevant curriculum. It is not uncommon to hold the student back a year and then ignore him/her as the curriculum moves forward without him/her. The other side to the problem is that parents of students at-risk often do not know how to advocate for their children or which channels to access in the school system. Parent communication is the first step to engaging a child in school. Furthermore, teachers need to be sensitive to the fact that students must sometimes negotiate literacy through bicultural or even tri-cultural experiences.

How Do We Meet the Challenge? (Purcell-Gates)

★ We must recruit and foster teachers who know, accept and celebrate the cultures of their students; they must see each student as a learner with unlimited potential.
★ We must provide teachers with the knowledge they need to be equipped in their classroom.
★ Teachers must be aware of the role that specific experience with and knowledge about written language plays in the process.
★ Instruction must recognize and appreciate what the child knows and does not know about print in all dimensions; diagnostic assessment of what needs to be learned is the key, not a judgment of deficiency.
★ In order for instruction to make sense, it must begin with each learner's language and the learner's world that is encoded with that language. This is the learner's primary Discourse.
★ Teachers must know and affirm the language and language knowledge of the different learners, as well as the cultures through which the learners have acquired the language.
★ We must give teachers the autonomy, authority and freedom to teach each child. Standardized curriculum and instructional practices put teachers into a moral quandary.
★ We need programs that focus on increasing the level and the degree of literacy in the homes of children.
★ We need to teach reading and writing holistically. Teaching reading and writing as decontextualized skills will not work.

Establishing a Literacy Committee

This committee may be made up of teachers, administrators, and interested parents and community members. Ideally, the committee will include representation of teachers from across subjects, grades and programs if it is to be truly authentic and effective. Some of the responsibilities of the Literacy Committee are:

★ To create a library of resources on literacy issues
★ To compile and summarize current information and research on literacy issues
★ To gather information on effective assessment and evaluation practices
★ To generate a list of best practices
★ To become familiar with the standards of the Grade Ten Test of Reading and Writing
★ To gather data regarding the ability/performance levels of individuals and groups students from a wide variety of sources
★ Identify literacy standards for students across each subject area
★ Identify factors in the school or community that affect student achievement in reading and writing
★ To gather date regarding the overall quality of program
★ To gather data regarding the needs of teachers (i.e. knowledge gaps, resources, implementation strategies, etc.)
★ Make decisions about how information will be shared with parents
★ Makes suggestions for professional development
★ Facilitate the sharing and implementation of best teaching practices across the curriculum
★ Provide opportunities for teachers to reflect on current practices and their impact on individual learners
★ Formulate focus questions to monitor student progress over time
★ Share successful ideas with other schools in the community/province

Planning for Success

Once a literacy committee has been established, there will be two focus points. The first will be short-term strategies to help teachers and students prepare for the Grade Ten Test. The second will be long-term strategies to improve programming and reach all segments of the population.

Short-Term Planning Strategies

★ create standard rubrics for paragraphs, reports, and essays for use across all subject areas
★ consult your board for resources and support – teachers are not expected to bear the burden alone – look for leadership — make sure every school is not reinventing the wheel
★ use TAP to support these initiatives
★ hold a mock exam and create a list of at-risk students; assess whether they need support with test-taking strategies, reading/writing strategies or both
★ implement a tip of the week across the curriculum
★ establish a list of reading and writing priorities across the curriculum which may be incorporated into and reinforced in each course
★ Encourage the use of the inquiry process across the curriculum

Long-Term Planning Strategies

★ Become familiar with the various members of the community and how literacy is used in the community
★ Work with the community to promote literacy in the home
★ Raise the expectations for students at-risk; do not water down the curriculum
★ Create school-wide programming which is inclusive, student-centred and responsive to individual needs
★ Work with elementary schools to establish goals and strategies for long-term, individualized planning for students
★ Establish community partnerships to take advantage of literacy and cultural programs in the community
★ Establish community partnerships to provide opportunities for students to see the relevance of literacy issues (i.e., have students read to seniors or younger children)

Methods of Collecting Data

From Teachers:

★ Questionnaires
★ Surveys
★ Checklists

Topics:

★ Instructional strategies
★ Standards
★ Expectations
★ Resources
★ Assessment and evaluation practices
★ Current challenges

★ Past successes

From Students:

★ Anecdotal information
★ Observation
★ Standardized test results (feedback from EQAO)
★ Academic assessments
★ Grades
★ Performance patterns
★ Writing samples
★ Portfolios
★ Videotapes
★ Interviews
★ Student surveys
★ Family surveys

The following charts may be helpful to teacher in assessing the focus on literacy in each subject area and classroom.

Reading Analysis Tools

Cloze Tests

★ pre-made Cloze Tests are usually available on computer programs such as the Academy of Reading, in the English and Special Education departments, and at the board

★ to make your own test, select a piece of grade-appropriate text (approx. 250 words)

★ use something high interest/low vocab for weaker readers (i.e., do not insult them with childish materials)

★ omit every fifth word and replace it with a blank

★ use 50 blanks (for a score out of 50)

★ results:

40% or less correct	frustration level
40-60% correct	instructional level
60% or more correct	independent level

Alternative Reading Assessment

★ informal and quick

★ recommended length:

Grade	words
1-2	25-50 words
3-4	50-75
5-6	75-100
7-8	100-150
9 -	150-200

★ if you are assess students in a Locally Developed course, use 65-100 words

★ use something high interest/low vocab for weaker readers (i.e., do not insult them with childish materials)

★ ask students comprehension questions

★ results:

Oral Reading	Comprehension	Level
99% accuracy	90% accuracy	Independent
95%	75%	Instructional
difficulty	70% or less	Frustration

Other Indicators of Comprehension:

★ paraphrasing (look for sequencing skills)

★ making predictions about text

★ present students with scrambled stories and look at the use of logical ordering

Miscellaneous Tips:
★ use the results of more than one type of reading assessment to get an accurate picture of student ability
★ read the OSR for past assessments
★ use other reading inventories if available
★ do formal assessments (i.e. WRAT, K-TEA, PPVT, etc.) if necessary

Informal Writing Assessment:

Provide students with a visual stimulus such as a photograph and ask them to write a story based on the image. Use the criteria on the following page to assess the level of ideation using the criteria on the next page. Use the chart to check off areas of mastery/concern. Reassess student writing intermittently throughout the course.

	Name	Level	Grammar & Punctuation	Sentence Structure	Paragraph Structure	Introduction Conclusion	Editing Process
1							
2							
3							
4							
5							
6							
7							
8							
9							
10							
11							
12							
13							
14							
15							
16							
17							
18							

Written Language Analysis				
Student:	Mechanics: (spelling; grammar; punctuation; sentence structure)	Handwriting: (spatial orientation; directionality; letter formation; speed of work)	Vocabulary: (specific or non-specific ; simple; concise; descriptive; imaginative)	Story Structure: (sequencing; connection of ideas; organization; introduction/con-clusion; sentence variety)

Teaching to Literacy

> *"Most high school teachers, including English teachers, are not trained to teach reading. Even those content area teachers who have taken preservice or inservice reading courses generally avoid incorporating literacy practices into their lessons (O'Brien & Stewart. 1992: Vacca & Vacca, 1996)." (Fischer, 326-7)*

Remedial reading programs must incorporate the following components if they are to succeed in raising reading levels and in providing other benefits to at-risk students (Fischer, 327):

★ Students must be at least minimally motivated to improve their reading
★ Students should receive daily reading practice
★ Assignments should be tailor made for each student with an emphasis on direct, explicit instruction
★ Adult volunteers, peer tutors, and the teacher should provide as much one-to-one tutoring as possible
★ There should be opportunities for verbal sharing as well as writing and publishing
★ Students should read to younger children regularly
★ Materials should be at an appropriate level and hold students' interest

Finding resources that are suitable and affordable can be a challenge. The following strategies may be helpful:

★ Borrowing books from local libraries and other schools to curb costs
★ Ask for donations of old books from families and teachers
★ Use newspapers (day old ones are free!; ask staff to bring in their old newspapers and magazines)
★ Try using comic strips which relate to the topic at hand
★ Magazines which cater specifically to students' interests are effective
★ Use students' textbooks to teach reading strategies; also, try linking the topics in texts to recent and relevant articles in the newspaper to deepen students' understanding

Tutor's Lesson Plans

Tutors can be a useful and cost-effective way to meet the needs of students at-risk. One strategy that is particularly useful when it comes to providing reading support is the use of a **Tutor Lesson Plan** (adapted from Fischer, 331) **(see page 68)**. The student is assigned to a tutor who then becomes familiar with the areas of need as well as the areas of interest of the student. The tutor's role is to facilitate the reading process/experience using feedback from the student and the teacher that is recorded on the form. Once the teacher has filled in the two boxes at the top of the form, the form may be reproduced for daily/weekly activities and only the lined sections need to be filled in. This tool promotes the ongoing communication necessary to promote student development. It may be time and energy-consuming at first, however, once the process has been worked through a couple of times, it can be a very effective way of monitoring student progress, as well as the quality of tutoring that is going on.

Tutor's Lesson Plan

Date: _____

Student: _____ Tutor: _____

Areas of Need:

Areas of Interest:

Activity:

_____

_____

Strategies Used:

_____

_____

_____

Effectiveness of Strategies:

_____

_____

Progress of Student:

_____

_____

Next Steps:

_____

_____

Literacy Strategies for the Classroom

★ set explicit expectations for each student in your classroom
★ read and write frequently
★ tell students when they are reading and when they are writing
★ teach metacognitive skills
★ teach reading strategies in the context of daily readings (e.g. highlighting important information; skimming; scanning, etc.)
★ see mistakes as part of the learning process
★ use reciprocal teaching practices where students ask you comprehension questions
★ have students teach the reading skills they have mastered; this boosts self-esteem and frees the teacher up to work with others
★ emphasize formative assessment of reading and writing skills
★ provide authentic opportunities for reading and writing
★ teach reading and writing in different contexts
★ involve students in the design of activities
★ only teach reading and writing strategies in the context of student reading and writing
★ take into consideration the student's attitude toward reading and writing when planning activities
★ use student's writing to practice reading
★ expose students to a variety of texts
★ draw students' attention to the style and format of different texts
★ read to the class
★ encourage and validate personal responses
★ teach student the language of tests across the curriculum
★ teach students test-taking strategies across the curriculum
★ teach the language of math
★ explain the obvious
★ emphasize process
★ encourage reading for personally meaningful reasons
★ make writing materials available in the classroom so that writing is fun and easier to approach
★ do not discourage inventive spellings, especially when the spellings derive from the phonics of the child's first language or dialect; this is part of the process of learning the patterns of language
★ readers must be able to relate on a content and a word level to the texts you use during instruction
★ teach about the culture of literacy as well as about the language of print; these must be experienced as a whole; be explicit; do not take it for granted that students have this knowledge
★ hold lunch hour remediation sessions
★ hold workshops for students and parents who are concerned about literacy issues

A Word About Reading Software Programs

There are a number of reputable reading software programs available such as *Autoskills' Academy of Reading*. Such programs require students to master a series of subskills and can be effective for students who would benefit from regimented exposure to language. ESL students tend to make the most progress in these programs as they benefit from the focus on phonetic units. However, the success of the program will be limited for those students whose language ability is affected by disabilities or general learning problems. Similarly, some students respond to the computer-oriented learning and others become bored quite quickly. These factors should be taken into consideration when purchasing software resources and in the design of a balanced literacy program. Ultimately, the child's literacy levels can only be improved through meaningful interaction with texts.

Home Practices Which Promote Literacy

★ Do not present reading as a punishment with the reward of watching television when they are done; treat it as a worthwhile family activity or a reward in and of itself
★ Read to children
★ Take turns reading aloud
★ Set aside 20-30 minutes per day to share reading time
★ Listen to your child read
★ Check for basic comprehension by asking questions (Who, What, When, Where, How, Why)
★ Ask your child to summarize what they have read
★ Discuss the meaning of new vocabulary words or look them up together
★ Ask your child to make connections and comparisons to between what they are reading and their life, movies they have seen and other books they have read
★ Ask your child to make predictions about what will happen next in the text
★ make reading material available in the home and ensure it is at the appropriate level
★ encourage your child to read what interests them (even comics!)
★ show interest in what they are reading

- ★ take your children to the library; help them get a library card; help them find books on their interests and hobbies
- ★ ask your school to send home a recommended reading list
- ★ ask your schools to provide guidelines on how to use newspapers and magazines to encourage reading
- ★ order subscriptions to your child's favourite magazine

Is My Classroom Literacy Literate?

A THOUGHTFUL INVENTORY FOR EDUCATORS

Reading is one of the major ways by which we expect students to learn in our subject area.

Writing is the main way in which we ask students to express their learning. Consider your classroom resources and daily practices to support reading and writing by completing the following inventory.

A. Is my classroom "reading ready"?	Yes	No
For this course, students will be required to read the following: ☐ A textbook? ☐ Articles from newspaper or magazine? ☐ Internet information? ☐ Maps, charts, or other graphic representations? ☐ Other _____		
Have I determined the readability of my classroom materials? ☐ Will some students have difficulty reading and gaining meaning from any of these materials? ☐ Have I considered ways to support them? ☐ Do I recognize the reading skills which I assume my students are capable of using with my course reading materials? ☐ Have I built activities into my daily pedagogy which will assist students with the reading skills which my subject materials require?		
Have I considered the vocabulary issues which may provide difficulty for all or some of the students in my classes? ☐ Do I have strategies in place to support students in learning the meaning of the vocabulary in my subject area? ☐ Do I have strategies in place to support students in learning the spelling of the vocabulary in my subject area, i.e. identifying roots, prefixes, suffixes?		
Am I aware of the unique features of the text(s) I use which make it user and reading friendly? ☐ Do I provide students with any assistance in "navigating" the various text features which may assist them to find and understand the material?		
Do I provide time in class each day for students to read, e.g., perhaps to respond to questions, to make summaries? ☐ Do I read aloud to students from the texts used in my subject? ☐ Do I model for students the thinking process of determining which information is most crucial for responding to questions or for making summaries?		

B. Is my classroom writing friendly?	Yes	No
1. For this course, students will be required to write: ☐ Answers to questions? ☐ "notes"? ☐ summaries of textbook or research material? ☐ Reports or procedures? ☐ Explanations or persuasive pieces? ☐ Explanatory answers to test or exam questions? ☐ Journals or diaries? ☐ Other _____		
2. Have I clearly defined my writing expectations for this course: ☐ For myself? ☐ For my students? ☐ Are they appropriate to the year and type of course and its content? ☐ Do my expectations match the Ministry curriculum document for the subject?		
3. Do I provide students with models or exemplars of the types of writing that I expect? ☐ Do I do some personal modeling of writing forms on the blackboard or overhead to "walk" students through the process of writing these forms? ☐ Do I provide opportunities for students to de-construct the writing forms and to re-construct them so that they can understand how they go together? ☐ Do I support student attempts with "templates" for more complex writing forms?		
4. Do I provide time in class for students to engage in subject-appropriate writing every day, e.g., answering textbook questions, taking notes, drafting reports or procedures? ☐ Do these writing tasks enhance and extend the classroom learning, subject-specific vocabulary, and concepts being developed?		
5. Do I help my students to understand the importance to clear writing of observing the "conventions" or spelling, punctuation, sentence structure, paragraph development, and appropriate level of language? ☐ Do I provide visual support around the classroom for difficult spelling? ☐ Do I provide opportunities for students to read each other's writing so that they develop their sense of audience and the need for clarity? ☐ Do I provide opportunities for students to engage in revising, editing, and proofreading drafts of a piece of writing, individually or with others?		

Adapted from *Contacts: Teaching Communication Across the Curriculum*, OSSTF, 1997

Literacy-Based Tasks in Various Subject Areas

Subject	Reading Tasks 📖	Writing Tasks ✎
The Arts: Art Drama Music		
English/ Languages		
Family Studies		
Geography		

History		
Mathematics		
Physical and Health Education		
Science		
Technical Studies		

Typical Literacy-based Tasks in Various Subject Areas

Subject	Reading Tasks 📖	Writing Tasks ✏	Oral & Visual ✍ Communication
The Arts – Art Dance Drama Music	Research on art in everyday life • Research on periods & forms • Critical works • Research into lives of musicians, artists, dramatists, dancers • Sheet music – notation, dynamic & tempo marks • Slides, films	• Critical analysis (deconstruction) of artwork or dramatic elements • Biography or summary • Monologue based on a character, scenes/short plays • Concert or play review • Learning logs, reflective journals • Lyric writing	• Slide presentation on artist's work • Performance, readings improvisations • Research-based presentation or seminar • Posters, tickets • Costume, set design • Independent Study • Lesson/workshop for younger students • Music appreciation • Group work
Business Studies	Analysis of case studies Text material	• Written business plan • Notes/summaries from text • Transcription and letter composition • Logs, reports	• Sales presentation • Interview role play • Group work
English/Languages	Novels, drama, poetry, short stories, essays Newspapers, magazine articles, advertisements, television shows, films	• Essays/stories: narrative, descriptive, expository • Editorial • Poetry, journals • Book reports • Deconstructions of advertisements, TV shows, radio formats	• Seminar presentations • Dramatic & choral readings • Individual/paired research-based presentations • Group work • Video of commercial or TV mini-drama
Family Studies	Text material Research on specific topics Instructions (recipes, patterns) Floor plans	• Notes/summaries from text, articles • Observation journals, surveys, menu planning • Position papers	• Research-based presentations • Group work

Geography	Text material Interpretation of charts, diagrams, photographs Inquiry model research process Magazine or newspaper article	• Notes/summaries from text, articles • Letters, editorials, travelogues • Position papers, persuasive writing • Action Plan	• Posters • Displays • Independent Study presentation • Slides, videos • Group work
History	Text material Periodicals, charts, documents, encyclopedias Biographies	• Notes/summaries from text • Book report • Analytical research essay • Diary entries, charts	• Debate, role play, seminar • Individual research-based presentation • Group work
Mathematics	Text instructions Word problems Biography	• Survey questions for data gathering • Analysis and interpretation of data • Mathematical sentences to word sentences • Reflective journals	• Posters, displays • Graphs, charts • Group work
Physical and Health Education	Rules for various sports/games Health information – articles, text material	• Action plans for personal health • Diaries, e.g., of foods eaten or activities • Reflective journals	• Clear communication of instructions and safety warnings • Purposeful dialogue during games • Poster, displays on health lifestyles
Science	Finding information in text Interpretation of charts/diagrams Biographies of famous scientists or accounts of scientific discoveries	• Summaries of text, responses to text questions • Note taking from lectures • Lab reports • Book reviews or summaries • Research report • Recording and analyzing data • Graphing data	• Seminars • Debates, role play around issues (fact vs. opinion/emotion) • Group work • Independent study presentation • Issue-based poster • "Explain your experiment" poster
Technical Studies	Text material Periodicals, manuals Tables, charts, symbolic diagrams	• Notes/summaries from text • Instructions • Reports, descriptions • Records, logs	• Safety poster • Demonstrations • Design brief • Computer tutorials

*adapted from *Contacts: Teaching Communication Across the Curriculum,* OSSTF 1997

Chapter 5   Curriculum Design for STARs

Introduction

Teaching is a process not a product. And while teaching requires the implementation of curriculum it also embodies a philosophy which drives our teaching. In order for all students to learn, teachers must have a broad understanding of the learner and a whole vision of the child. Learning is a process which occurs through the natural feedback of the environment. Learning is not a mechanical process. As a result, it is necessary to look at curriculum design from a broader perspective. The following section is meant to outline and highlight the key principles of curriculum design.

Curriculum design includes three main components:

The **content** that is included (and excluded)
The **sequence** in which the course is presented
The learning **activities** which are used to put the course content in context

Each of these components shapes each student's educational experience. If any of these components are in conflict with a student's socio-cultural background or learning style, that student's success will be limited. Hence, the need exists to develop content that relates to the student's current interests and life experiences and that is compatible with their learning styles.

Learning is an integrative process that involves the whole child. The **intellectual, interpersonal** and **intrapersonal dynamics** of the student need to be reflected in the curriculum. Such a holistic curriculum is **experiential** in nature and follows the transformation model of learning.

The goal of experiential learning is to connect with what is meaningful in students' lives. Experiential curriculum provides a meaningful context in which to learn skills and concepts. The challenge for teachers is to balance the increasing demands of a skill and content-based curriculum with the experiential needs of the students.

The **transmission model** of learning reflects the traditional teacher-centred classroom where the curriculum is presented to students in a top-down method of teaching.

> *"Wise teachers do not give up. They recognize that sometimes students may appear to be making little progress, but they do not give up...for methods that have the appearance of quick learning. Generations of students who take years of history and forget it all because it was rote memorization of names and dates, or those who take years of foreign language classes and can't speak or write, tell us that it would be better to encourage learning deeply through many activities that apply acquired skills and knowledge. Do not be fooled into thinking that rote learning and the rewards of temporary high test scores will make for lifelong retention and caring." (Nagel, 123)*

The **transaction model** of learning embodies more interaction between students, with the teacher, and with the curriculum. While this model is more effective than the rote learning methods of the transmission model, it still tends to focus on the cognitive domain of the child. A focus on memorization tends to result in the recurring phenomena of students forgetting the bulk of course content shortly after exams.

The **transformation model** of learning incorporates mind, body and spirit and focuses on making deep connections within the student and to the community. Incorporating this model of teaching/learning promotes lasting memory of learning experiences and therefore, the knowledge, skills and concepts embedded in those experiences.

Overview of the Three Basic Models of Curriculum Design:

Model	TRANSMISSION $O \Rightarrow O$	TRANSACTION $O \Leftrightarrow O$	TRANSFORMATION
Typical Instructional Methods	• Socratic Teaching	• Multi-modal delivery • Inquiry model • Co-operative Learning • Discussion	• Experiential learning • Reflection • Use of imagery • And narrative • Focus on making connections between mind/body/soul
Organization	• Subject-based • Autocratic	• Thematic • Democratic	• Student-centred • Humanistic • Holistic
Learning Environment	• Controlled • Seating arranged in rows	• Seating arranged in groups or pairs	• Open • Inviting • Dynamic • Circular seating arrangement
Predominant Teaching Style	• Auditory	• Multiple intelligences and learning styles	• Focus is on fostering connections inside and outside the person/classroom

Teachers may want to take advantage of the moment of silence provided during morning announcements, or create their own. Try using a combination of breathing exercises and thoughts of the day to help focus their students on current themes, topics of study or major events in the news. Encourage students to create and share their own meditations for the day. This entry point to the day will better enable students to make connections in their learning.

Values Education

The new curriculum does not incorporate values into its lists of expectations. Nonetheless, educators know that values education plays an important part in the learning environment. Teachers may draw on their own creativity to find ways to incorporate values into the daily curriculum.

It is important for teachers to make connections between the knowledge and skills being learned in the classroom and their relevance to students' lives and the community. This approach helps to integrate values in our education process. This approach may be particularly useful in curriculum areas like science and geography where technology and the environment are under discussion. "Values are derived from realizing the fundamental connectedness between individuals; in other words, values are linked to relatedness. Positive values enhance or realize relatedness, and negative values foster separateness and paranoia...What is 'right' is that which helps maintain caring and relatedness." (Miller, The Holistic Curriculum, p. 26)

Regardless of the circumstances that pervade students' lives, a student's degree of educational success ultimately depends on the instructional experiences to which students are exposed and involved in. Below is a reflection on some of the most popular theories on learning:

Anti-Racist Education

Issues of racism in the classroom are often marginalized as a study unto itself. Anti-racist education embodies a positive, proactive and inclusive approach to curriculum design, rather than one that simply reacts to prejudice and stereotype along the way. While educators tend to be good at avoiding using texts that contain overt racism and prejudice, they often overlook the need to include multicultural texts. As a result, the curriculum often becomes void of meaning for many students whose socio-cultural backgrounds are not reflected in the curriculum.

Teachers should also look beyond the content used to the very instructional strategies and approaches that may or may not cater to the needs and styles of learners from different groups and communities.

The Hidden Curriculum

Through the educational process, we transmit cultural values in a way that is not always clearly revealed. Many of the tools teachers use, such as textbooks, comics and newspapers, are value-laden. Teachers should be mindful to what is being conveyed through the tools or strategies being used and they should be modified to ensure inclusivity or at least referenced to the value context of the material.

The Subskills Orientation

Much of the traditional curriculum uses a subskills orientation in which the learning process is broken down into a series of subtasks and taught in a sequential manner. This approach disregards the need for a relevant context, as well as the holistic nature of learning. It is important to provide opportunities for authentic and personally meaningful learning.

When a concept is about to be learned, allow students to experience it in its wholeness before attempting to teach its pieces. Singing the complete song before learning the notes, painting a bright picture comes before studying the colour wheel, hearing a total story comes before learning the words and sounds, watching the metamorphosis comes before learning its stages (Nagel, 89)

The Constructivist Approach

This approach is based on the idea that instruction begins with student knowledge and experiences. In order for curriculum to be meaningful and relevant students must be able to construct meaning from new information and relate new ideas to what they already know. They may then use this knowledge to draw inferences and conclusions. There is a heavy emphasis on concept development and problem solving. The constructivist approach focuses on the cognitive domain of the child.

Multiple Intelligences

Howard Gardner has identified eight types of intelligences that may be exhibited and incorporated into curriculum practices. They are: verbal/linguistic, logical/mathematical, interpersonal, intrapersonal, bodily/kinesthetic, musical, visual/spatial, and naturalist. This theory of intelligence and learning is cognitive in its orientation. Looking at multiple intelligences in the classroom enables us to see students learning 'differences' rather than disabilities. It also helps us to see how teaching and learning are inherently limited when we only use linguistic and logical modes of thinking.

Incorporating all of these modes of learning into the classroom will engage more learners. In fact, STARs often have hidden strengths that are brought to light when some of these alternative modes of learning are used. One useful activity is to have each student create a pie chart or poster of the different intelligences (leave space for other types, too) and create an image or symbol that expresses that intelligence. Students may also want to list famous people who embody each intelligence.

Emotional Intelligence

This popular term was coined by Daniel Goleman. In his book "Working with Emotional Intelligence" he highlights the importance of being literate when it comes to the emotional workings of ourselves and others. Goleman points out the positive relationship between our affective well-being and our success in education, relationships and careers. Helping students identify, express and relate their emotional experiences is an effective way of making the curriculum in your classroom more meaningful and promoting the growth of the whole child.

Learning Styles

There are three basic learning styles: visual, auditory and tactile. Incorporating these three styles into teaching will facilitate the learning of more students. Try to present all important concepts using all three styles. For example, when teaching about Shakespeare's Globe Theatre, use oral/written descriptions, visual images and try having students create a model. **See page 86** for a **Learning Style Quiz**.

Metacognitive Skills

It is important to make students aware of how they think, write, read, etc. Making the obvious obvious is an effective way of incorporating metacognitive skills into the learning process and teaching reading and writing strategies to those students who need them. Always teach these strategies in a meaningful context and not on their own. For example, as you are reading a passage together, use skimming and scanning.

Using metacognitive skills is particularly effective with students who have difficulty listening or paying attention. Work on creating awareness of students' inner process and encourage them to respond to internal cues more effectively (e.g., teach them about 'self-talk' and how to keep themselves on track by telling themselves to listen/focus).

Effective curriculum design

that promotes the success of all students includes:
- ★ A balance of content and process
- ★ A focus on higher-order thinking skills
- ★ Explicit teaching of learning and thinking strategies (meta-cognitive skills)
- ★ Making connections between academic content and students' prior knowledge and experiences (constructivist approach)
- ★ A focus on student strengths
- ★ Real-life learning applications
- ★ Role play

★ Making connections by having them reflect on hypothetical situations in the past, present and future
★ Peer tutoring to foster the development of academic and social skills
★ Authentic tasks and assessment and evaluation methods
★ Mixed-ability groupings
★ Co-operative learning

Planning Guidelines

★ Look at what the curriculum demands:
>   Overall expectations for each unit
>   What students need to succeed in the real world
>   What students need to succeed in future courses of study

★ Based on their needs, ask yourself:
>   a) What do you want every student to know?
>   b) What do you want most students to know?
>   c) What do you want a few students to know?

★ Look at the vocabulary/concepts associated with the content you will be teaching:
>   At what level of conceptualization are you looking?
>   Is it concrete or abstract?
>   Build a framework for the lesson/unit using this information.

★ Investigate what skills/knowledge the students have before you begin:
>   What assumptions have you made in terms of background knowledge?
>   Begin where they are.
>   Make instructional interventions as needed.

★ Plan lessons/sequence units:
>   Include oral, reading and writing performance activities which give everyone the opportunity to integrate concepts.

★ Clearly present the forms of evaluation from which students may choose:
>   Negotiate the terms of evaluation with students; be realistic.
>   Try developing a rubric together
>   If the evaluation methods are directly linked to lessons, students are more likely to strive to learn and meet the expectations laid out.

LEARNING STYLES QUIZ

Our actions can reveal the learning styles we are most comfortable with. If you look up a lot you are probably a visual learner; if you look side to side you are probably an auditory learner; if you use your hands a lot you are probably a hands-on (tactile) learner. Ask the following questions to your partner and mark their response with the following symbols:

↑   if they look up   Total: _____

→   if they look sideways or side to side   Total: _____

X   if they use their hands or gesture   Total: _____

QUESTIONS

_____   1. Is the main office north, south, west or east of our classroom?

_____   2. What is your favourite colour?

_____   3. Name a Thursday night TV show.

_____   4. Name a song with the word "love" in it.

_____   5. What is your favourite fast food?

_____   6. Which direction is Mexico?

_____   7. When you are opening a jar of jam, which way do you turn the lid?

_____   8. What colour is the uniform of the Toronto Maple Leafs'?

_____   9. Which is bigger, the CN Tower or the Eiffel Tower?

_____   10. Which side of the road do they drive on in England?

_____   11. What does $2 + 5 - 4$ equal?

_____   12. Who is the Prime Minister of Canada?

_____   13. Which hand do you write with?

_____   14. What is the first thing we hear on the announcements in the morning?

General Planning Tips:

★ Involve students
★ Find ways to connect students with the curriculum and ask students to make connections
★ Provide opportunities for success for all students

For a model of how to design curriculum using the overall expectations please **see pages 135-137** for **Course Rubrics for a Locally Developed English** course (ENG 14M) and page 127 for an explanation of how to use them.

Homework Strategies

Students at-risk tend not to do homework, and for very good reasons. If you do assign homework to them, it must be work which students can do on their own which is meaningful and relevant. Most students will not do 'busywork'. It is insulting to them and does not help them learn. When assigning homework, try structuring it as extensions of current units of study or independent study such as simple science experiments that can be tried at home. Offer homework as enrichment, bonus work or make it practical (e.g., find an example in the school/community) so that they can do it and feel part of the class. Ideally, homework assignments and schedules should be compatible with the routines and support available at home. Establish clear expectations regarding homework and help students see its connection to the curriculum and learning.

The **Homework Tracking Sheet** (page 89) and **Homework Record** (page 90) are useful tools for communicating with parents and keeping STARs on track. Students are responsible for writing down their homework in each class and having the teacher sign their entry, making positive/negative comments where appropriate. With some students, teachers may want to have them check in at the end of the day to ensure that the form is completed and signed. (Otherwise, they will need to find their teachers and fill it in properly.) At home, the parent will sign the sheet to indicate that all homework has been completed and will make comments as necessary.

Wise teachers hunt for success

Nagel (223

Homework Tracking Sheet

Date: _____

Class/Teacher	Homework/Comments	Teacher Sign.

Parent Signature: _____

Comments:

Homework Record

NAME:_____ DATE:_____

COURSE:_____

MY HOMEWORK FOR TONIGHT		TEACHER	PARENT
THINGS TO DO BEFORE STARTING ASSIGNMENT			
POSITIVE THINGS IN CLASS TODAY			
GOALS FOR TOMORROW			

COMMENTS:
 	
  Student –
  Teacher –
  Parent -			

COURSE:_____

MY HOMEWORK FOR TONIGHT		TEACHER	PARENT
THINGS TO DO BEFORE STARTING ASSIGNMENT			
POSITIVE THINGS IN CLASS TODAY			
GOALS FOR TOMORROW			

COMMENTS:
 	
  Student –
  Teacher –
  Parent -			

Unit Ideas

Students benefit most from learning activities that provide in-depth opportunities to explore ideas and master skills. Larger units and projects are preferable over short, skills-oriented activities. And if you find a topic or project idea that captures student interest, consider extending it in new and interesting ways. The context for learning is crucial. The following ideas have been used successfully in the past for the enjoyment and education of all students, but most notably, STARs:

> *...great teaching is not dependent upon fancy materials..."Give me a class of kids and a phone book and we'll do fine." (Nagel, 37)*

Language/Social Studies Focus

Toronto Star's "Conflict Resolution" insert
This free newspaper insert is full of adaptable ideas and resources for reading, writing, literary, media-related and discussion activities.

Wrestling Unit
This unit was designed around the popular WWF events and athletes and incorporated reading, writing, on-line/off-line research, discussion, surveys, interviews, presentation activities, etc. This unit is a great way to capture student interest (if applicable) at the beginning of the year.

Class Newspaper
This unit makes an excellent culminating activity for the year. Each student takes on a role and contributes to the creation of this media product. Issues of content, format, visuals, layout and design, headlines, etc. may be covered. Also, the heavy emphasis on editing becomes an authentic effort in this context. Try printing out copies of the entire paper and draft form, circling all errors that need editing and asking leading

questions regarding paragraph structure, headings, etc. Have students edit the work individually and then take it up as a class. Make editorial decisions together. Each student gets a copy of the product to take home at the end of the year. Printing the publication in colour also makes it more rewarding. This is a great finale.

Comic Strips

Comics are a great activity for use across subject areas, especially where social commentary is at the centre of the curriculum. Teachers can provide collections and samples of comic strips or students can create their own incorporating characters from the community around them. These media products may be used to teach perspective, story-line, narrative, historical events, social issues, political issues, bias and prejudice, etc.

Children's Book Creation

Students should reflect on the popular texts of their childhood and examine them for stereotypes and biases. Fairy tales and contemporary children's books also serve as good models. Discussion of the elements of children's literature and the importance of audience may be incorporated. When students have published their own writing and illustrating (these roles may be shared in the class, depending on student confidence and ability levels) they should share them with younger children in the community and local elementary schools.

Personal Mythology

Focusing on mythological stages and events inherent in students' own lives can enliven a mythology unit. Traditional texts can be brought in where appropriate. Popular stories from different media (i.e., television, film, cartoons, etc.), and even urban myths, may be incorporated. The end product may take the form of a comic strip, story, video, etc. Research projects on modern heros (e.g., Martin Luther king, Jr. are a good extension.)

Cross-Curricular Focus

Millennium Project

Use this overriding theme to teach students concepts like time, history, technology, inventions, family, education, the environment, the aging process, etc. The unit should place students' lives at the centre of these concepts and foster connections to past, present and future milestones and turning points in society.

News Publications

Newspapers and magazines are good source of resources, lesson plans and even workshops (contact your local paper of choice) on all subjects. **Web Addresses** are available on pages 175-187.

Music Project

Do a series of lessons on the history of music. Invite your music teacher in to do a presentation on an area of interest. Create a timeline which incorporates music from different cultures. Each student picks a genre of interest. (Working in pairs also works.) Students research, write about, and present on one genre. All presentations must include visuals/demonstrations, etc. The results are quite creative and entertaining.

Poetry Meets Art

A poetry unit can be made tactile and visual by having classes interpret other classes' poems through art. The artists can present their interpretations and bring students' words to life. (This could also be done within a single class so that each student has a chance to interpret a poem and create a visual piece).

Poetry Meets Science & Geography

Students can create poetry in response to first-hand experiences, experiments and concepts related to the physical world we live in. Likewise, students can generate poems at the beginning of the course (or each unit) on those natural phenomena that fascinate them the most (e.g., clouds, lightning, motion, the seasons, etc.). These poems can then be used to frame new units of study to which they relate.

Interdisciplinary and Intercultural Connections Through Art

Numerous lesson plans and curriculum ideas are available online at www.artsednet.getty.edu

Reaching Out to Others

Students can brainstorm a focus for a collaborative group effort that reflects what they believe their school culture to be. For example, an Alternative Education class, in the spirit of inclusion, saw a need for reaching out to the Developmentally Disabled students in the school. Therefore, the Alternative Ed. students researched the various developmental disabilities of the students in that class. They interviewed teachers, nurses, youth workers, and parents, from a comprehensive list of questions that were compiled after extensive library research. The Alternative Class began to spend time with their 'subjects' and, with the aid of a Physical Education teacher, used their collective knowledge to create workout plans for the students, so that their motor skills would be enhanced. The Alt Ed. students took photos of their new friends, and made display boards so that the larger school community could share in what they learned. Art students created visual reflections of their interpretation of this special friendship, and the artwork ended up on display at the local Board of Trade for the community to share. The Toronto Star **(see pages 29-30)** featured this collaborative effort, and then the CBC did a segment that was featured Canada wide, on the success of the students' efforts towards inclusivity.

Using the Story Model with Students At-Risk

> *Joseph Campbell (1988) noted that in this age of alienation and fragmentation, young people have a difficult decision to make and are responding with choices leading them to drugs, alcohol, and suicide. He pointed out that ancient people had myths, story, and ritual to guide them. He lamented that today we have no central story and called for the creation of a modern one. (Drake, 7)*

The story model of curriculum integration is an effective method for meeting the needs of students at-risk. It is highly student-centred, and offers a flexible and authentic method of teaching concepts. Furthermore, it actively involves students in the analysis of past and present society, and, most importantly, in the creation of a vision for the future.

The story model can be used across the curriculum with almost any topic and provides a meaningful, real-life context for learning. It incorporates themes as well as the inquiry model. But perhaps its most valuable characteristic is the way in which it facilitates insight into the way we perceive our society and ourselves.

The story model is also empowering in that it promotes the creation of a new worldview, based on students' personal stories. The story model transforms the curriculum into a meaningful learning and living experience. Furthermore, it promotes a highly active way of learning and is particularly conducive to the flexibility of alternative programming.

Sample topics include trees, the sun, automobiles, animals, fashion, body language, music, religious holidays and themes, gender issues, constitutional issues, poverty, conflict resolution, etc. Each of these topics can be used to create webs which touch on media, social, cultural, economic, environmental, political, legal, technological, global and societal issues.

Incorporating the Story Model in Your Classroom
(Adapted from Drake, 5)

1) Choose a topic -- the more specific the better (e.g., trees).
2) A visual of the model (including the old story, the present story, the ideal and projected story, personal stories and the new story) will be useful to refer to as students progress through each stage of the process. Similarly, the class may want to come up with an image, word or symbol which represents the topic in each of these story phases.
3) Use the personal story as a way of knowing: have students reflect on what the topic means to them by recounting an experience they have had with the given topic (e.g., climbing a tree).
4) Explore the topic in its real life context. Students will begin to make connections between the topic and its real-life context. (tree-cutting; pulp and paper industry; housing development, etc.) Incidentally, their personal stories as to the meaning of the topic will also be put in question.
5) Ask the question "How did we get here?" (i.e., how did trees become threatened?) The focus on the past as an "old story" may be quite recent or may go back far in time. However, since the past is being presented as a story, the narrative of events will be laden with values (e.g. independence, autonomy, achievement, power, consumerism, materialism, greed, etc.).
6) In groups, create a vision of the past and then of the present (i.e., how trees were seen/treated in the past compared to how they are seen/treated in the present). Using this framework enables students to make connections between the past and the present and to begin to create a meaningful place for themselves in that narrative. The connections which are fostered are far deeper than with traditional textbook learning.
7) At this point the focus of lessons turns to the future. The first step is to examine the outcome of continuing in the same pattern which has led to the present state of affairs (the projected vision). This may be done through a creative writing or visualization exercise where students imagine themselves living in the context of the old story (past and present events) in 20 years (e.g., a treeless planet without oxygen). The second step is to imagine an ideal future (the ideal vision) (tree-lined streets, abundant forests, etc.). Keep in mind that students may have different ideals.

8) This stage involves the creation of a new story. Collaborative groupings of different sizes should be used. This stage, while challenging, should not be directed by the teacher. However, nurturing values such as love, caring, compassion, co-operation, collaboration, respect and equality will likely emerge. This story should connect the present narrative to the ideal.

9) The action stage asks students to connect the new story to their personal story. After students have identified the values which are necessary for the future story they will need to generate ideas on how to act on them. This may involve interaction with the community (e.g., letter-writing to the government) or individual commitments to change personal behaviours (e.g., plant a tree; clean up a park, recycle paper, etc.).

10) At this point students may choose a related area of interest they would like to explore either individually or as a group. Students should generate a list of questions with which to frame their study. Research, field visits and other inquiry activities will be the focus of this phase. Resources include newspapers, magazines, the Internet, the library and people in the field.

11) At this stage students will present/demonstrate their versions of the old and new story for their piece of the puzzle. In this final stage students will see the patterns and themes across the various subtopics and will be better able to envision and see the need for a new story.

For further ideas, consult Developing an Integrated Curriculum Using the Story Model by S. Drake.

Trials, temptations, disappointments — all these are helps instead of hindrances, if only one uses them rightly. They not only test the fibre of character, but strengthen it. Every conquered temptation represents a new fund of moral energy. Every trial endured and weathered in the right spirit makes a soul nobler and stronger than it was before. (James Buckham)

TRIBES© and STARs

(by Beverley Madigan, Head of Computer Studies, YRDSB)

The word TRIBES© initially conjures up confusing mental images and ideas as students, parents, and teachers come together to dialogue about its potential role in education. Does it exclude specific groups of people? Is it just another add-on to existing Ontario curriculum? Do I have to receive specialized training? Most importantly, how can it benefit youth at risk?

TRIBES© is not a curriculum or a set of group activities. It is not about fixing kids or implementing generic band-aid quick fix prevention programs on school violence, drug and alcohol abuse, and suicide. TRIBES© is about transforming the school environment with a common vision, language and set of practices about how the human brain learns. It is a step-by-step process of maintaining a learning community inside and outside the walls of the local school. It is a human development framework that fosters resiliency and evokes our students' innate potentials. TRIBES© is grounded in educational research on human relations, behavioural science, brain-compatible and co-operative learning and teaching, multiple intelligences, thematic instruction, and conflict resolution.

TRIBES© was conceived, by Jeanne Gibb, a classroom teacher, approximately thirty years ago to assist youth at-risk through the creation of positive peer groups that valued people over things. The students in these cooperative learning groups developed character attributes such as respect and responsibility and were taught to reflect on their learning experiences and celebrate each other's uniqueness in this multicultural society. Gibb (1995) says, "Throughout the years people who have experienced this caring community building process kept saying: This is like being in a family...not a team but a tribe. People appreciated the social support, the respect for individual differences, and the sense of belonging that are inherent in tribal societies. The word 'team' never fit because it denoted competition. TRIBES© symbolized the affection and caring that so many of us in Western society long for today." Hence TRIBES© was born.

TRIBES© is thriving today in both elementary and secondary school communities throughout Australia, Canada, Europe and the United States as a caring teaching and learning process. With successful implementation it becomes an on-going culture within the school community, sustained through its learning systems: family, school, peer and neighbourhood. These learning systems must foster the following protective factors (Bonnie Benard, 1991) in order for any child to overcome life's misfortunes.

1. caring and supportive relationships
2. positive and high expectations
3. opportunities for meaningful discussions

TRIBES© moves our youth from a state of hopelessness to one of hopefulness through its inculcation of these protective factors. Research shows that students from communities that use TRIBES© have the greatest opportunity to develop life-long abilities of:

★ social competence and globally accepted character attributes
★ problem solving skills
★ autonomy
★ sense of purpose with a belief in a bright future

(Benard 1991) & (Gibb 1995),(Werner and Smith 1992).

This is what we want for our youth at-risk. There are many historical accounts of young people who did not feel included within a group so they acted out or dropped out. Their fundamental human need of feeling connected to their environment and being capable of performing something useful were not being met. TRIBES© works for students by helping them to solve problems, contribute in a positive way and respectfully reach out to everyone. This is why elementary and secondary schools report a significant decline in discipline problems within the first six months of using the TRIBES© process within classrooms. Even teachers say they have more time to teach as they are spending less time managing the students' inappropriate behaviours. The facts are evident, the question becomes: How can we actualize the TRIBES© process in educational institutions so all high-risk students benefit?

The TRIBES© mission is to create an environment infused with protective factors where students can grow and each one has the knowledge, skills and resiliency to be successful in a fast-paced world. This mission can be accomplished as the school community engages all teachers, administrators, students and families in working collaboratively as a learning community that is dedicated to caring and supporting, active participation and positive expectations for all students. Unlike many cooperative learning interactions, the TRIBES© approach involves all groups of people in long-term membership in small communities (tribes: groups of 4-6 members); parents in classroom groups, teachers in faculty groups and students in co-operative learning tribes. This structure provides inclusion within any group of peers no matter the age, culture or stage of personal development. Appreciation for each person's uniqueness as defined by the Human Rights Code is assured with TRIBES©. (Gibb, 1995). Let's be clear, whatever happens at the student-level must also be happening elsewhere in the school community. Adults need to model the skills and behaviours we expect of our children. TRIBES© must be integrated into everything we do at the staff and community levels. This can be achieved at staff and school council meetings, clubs and organization get-togethers, in the school halls and office and in the surrounding community. To successfully implement the TRIBES©

philosophy and methodology in your school community:

★ Recognize it is a process, not something undertaken alone. Incorporating TRIBES© in to your school culture takes time, patience and dedication. This will keep you grounded throughout the journey.
★ Connect with the community. Involve people at all levels: students, parents, staff, administrators and local neighbourhood role models.
★ Experience TRIBES© for yourself. Visit TRIBES© schools (e.g., Wexford Collegiate and Cedar Brooke Junior Public School in Toronto)
★ Examine the research. Read and discuss the documents in the Bibliography with your school community members.
★ Acquire TRIBES© training from a certified professional. (Contact Beverley Madigan: YRDSB or Denise Overall: TDSB). Staff development is a vital part of the process.

Contact www.tribes.com for more information.

Chapter 6   Instructional Strategies for STARs

Overview

While Secondary School Reform does not create opportunities for adaptive instruction, small efforts can be made, depending on the resources and support available in the classroom. Otherwise, STARs will be a growing population.

Once teachers have considered the whole child and the curriculum, they must look at the techniques and strategies they will use to instruct. "Some teachers are more likely than others to address the diverse learning needs of students who are exceptional [and] at risk." (Jordan, 91) One of the best ways to increase the effect of instruction is to maximize the amount of direct instructional time spent with individual students. "By coordinating ancillary and volunteer personnel to help individual groups of pupils, and to manage the flow of activities, then engaged time of pupils on learning materials can effectively be doubled...[and the teacher is] freed to devote more time to individual pupils." (Thomas (1985, 1986, 1987) in Jordan, 90)

The focus of teaching in a mainstreamed classroom tends to be on the instructional procedures conventionally used in that placement. Instruction is a dynamic process which needs to respond to the needs of the group and individuals in the group. Traditional teaching practices emphasize students' abilities to met pre-established instructional practices, whereas adaptive instruction responds to the needs of all learners in a seamless, fluid and dynamic fashion. The following instructional behaviours of teachers were shown to have the greatest benefits for student achievement and self-concept (adapted from Rosenshine (1983) in Jordan, 92):

1. Reviewing:
   a) the previous day's work, and reteaching, if needed, and
   b) weekly, monthly and end-of-unit reviews;
2. Allowing student to practise:
   a) in class, and using this to monitor students' understanding, and
   b) independently, out of class;
3. Giving frequent, detailed feedback and corrections. Feedback and reinforcers are most effective when they are positive and therefore enhance the pupil's self-concept.

The following section outlines effective strategies for working with students at-risk in every classroom.

Teachers who promote the success of all students:

★ See themselves as facilitators of learning, not as deliverers of content
★ Look for the potential of each student preconceived labels associated with that student and focus on their strengths
★ Welcome integration into their classrooms
★ Value diversity in their classrooms and see heterogeneous groups of students as a resource not a hindrance
★ Adjust the content and complexity of questions and statements to the content and form of the student's replies (Jordan, 91)
★ Interact with students at-risk as frequently as they do with other students (Jordan, 91)
★ Build on the background experiences of students and use that foundation to promote the learning of new knowledge and skills
★ Promote class collaboration in the planning, instruction, and assessment and evaluation of coursework
★ Use co-operative learning to promote collaboration and reduce feelings of alienation and competition
★ Refrain from using passive Socratic methods as their main teaching style
★ Rely less on listening activities
★ Provide more active learning activities
★ Use a variety of teaching strategies
★ Provide instruction in a variety of settings within and outside the school
★ Foster personal connections to the people in the class and the curriculum
★ Include the involvement of non-traditional teachers such as community members, mentors and race-sex role models from an array of backgrounds
★ Use parent tutors
★ Use peer tutors to support students individually or in groups
★ Integrate technology as a tool for instruction
★ Help students set and monitor individual learning goals
★ Use peer and self-assessment
★ Emphasize high expectations for all students
★ Praise at every opportunity
★ Recognize and acknowledge effort and growth

Accommodations

Accommodations are those strategies which promote student learning without changing the curriculum expectations of the course. **Please see pages 29-30 for the difference** between accommodations and modifications.) These strategies are most effective when they are incorporated into classroom planning, instruction, and assessment and evaluation practices. If accommodations are used out of the context of the immediate learning environment (i.e., in withdrawal settings) they are not as effective. The following is a list of effective and easy to implement accommodations that can be used across the curriculum.

Top Ten Accommodations to Help All Students Learn:
1. Put daily/weekly agenda on the board.
2. Use 'chalk and talk' (write key words/draw mindmaps, etc. while you talk).
3. Use visuals (diagrams, images, pictures, objects) to explain concepts.
4. On worksheets: bold key words; use 12 point font (minimum); double-space text; provide adequate room for responses; remember, white space is good
5. Chunk large assignments into smaller components and monitor work completion and check for understanding at each stage; provide feedback on work submitted.
6. Simplify vocabulary when necessary (especially on handouts); pre-teach vocabulary at the beginning of each lesson and post important terms around the room.
7. Break down and number instructions; provide a checklist if helpful to students.
8. Use concept mapping and charts to organize information.
9. Explain new concepts using concrete examples from real life.
10. Provide examples of excellent finished products.

Top Ten Teaching Tips to Help All Students Learn:

1. Make learning fun and engaging.
2. Repeat and review concepts daily.
3. Make the learning as hands-on and as engaging as possible (e.g., find out student strengths and incorporate them into lessons).
4. Provide reading material at the appropriate level and in an easy-to-read format.
5. Read texts as a class. Students should read aloud only when comfortable.
6. Help students recognize transferable skills which can be applied to new contexts (i.e., make generalizations, locate the main idea) and transfer them to new contexts.
7. Limit writing to short notes and provide worksheets that minimize writing (i.e. fill-in-the-blanks).
8. Use group work; students prefer this to working alone.
9. Provide structured review and give open-book tests. Have students flag key concepts ahead of time by placing labelled stickies on the edges of pages.
10. Limit tests to small units of study and provide opportunities for shorter, more authentic assessments.

A wise teacher learns to be a good listener...Spend time with the students who need you to listen. You can demonstrate your acceptance of who each student is by your willingness to give of yourself. Take the time to write down (or even tape-record) what your students say and reflect upon the words at a later time. You may be surprised at what you missed upon mere listening. Few words are necessary when you listen well, and students will learn that as time goes on, they need teachers comments less and less. They will become increasingly less dependent on the teacher's approval and rely more on their own. Join the students on their wavelengths; your receptivity shows a weakness that ends up being a strength in winning the situation for everyone. (Nagel, 83)

The Golden Rules of Teaching STARs

1) Do not rely on pre-packaged curricula that have not been customized to meet the needs of individual students. Textbooks will wreak havoc in your classroom.
2) You must reach them to teach them. Education is not useful or appreciated by these students unless it relates to them directly.
3) Emotional needs and development are more important than the skills these students bring to the classroom. The learning process must involve the whole child to be successful.
4) Students at-risk, are eager to please when they feel safe.
5) You will never be able to teach reading or math, etc. You must teach students how to read and how to do math. Treat the learning process as a language in and of itself.
6) You must teach students why they are learning a particular skill or concept and point out its relevance.
7) Always start with what students know.
8) Find ways to engage students in the learning process. If you want to motivate them intrinsically, choose topics they are passionate about.
9) Many students at-risk have poor memory skills (for social/emotional/cognitive reasons). Put strategies in place to reduce the effect of this fact on learning.
10) The learning environment needs to balance structure (for security) with freedom (for independence).
11) Instruction and assessment must be individualized to promote optimum success.
12) The most crucial skills must be taught across the curriculum.
13) Passive and aggressive behaviours may come from the same source of frustration - the inability to connect. Put inappropriate behaviour in perspective.
14) Teaching students at-risk is like surfing. If you catch a wave, stay on the board as long as possible. If you fall off, get back on and look for another wave.
15) Nothing promotes success like success.

Instructional Strategies

In telling one child that she or he is a great student, the best speller, or the top math student, you are closing doors to other students. Instead, use words that thank children for specific acts: "You must have worked hard to put such neatness and detail in your map." "The pear pictures in your story will make the first graders happy." "Thanks for including so many figures of speech in your poem". Encouraging words are true. (Nagel, 33)

Co-operative Learning

Co-operative learning, if planned and implemented in a manner which meets the needs of the students in the class, is an excellent method of promoting student involvement, student success and a sense of community in the classroom.

William Glasser is long-time advocate of making the classroom a community. Glasser believes that using learning teams in classrooms is one way to satisfy the human need to belong. A learning team consists of one high achieving student, a low achieving student and two or three average students. The team works together to achieve a group goal. Glasser claims that the low achiever is difficult to recognize in the group because he/she is more productive in the group context. (Miller, The Holistic Curriculum, 139)

Roy Smith (1987), a teacher who uses cooperative learning in his classroom, believes that teachers should follow these guidelines for co-operative learning (Miller, The Holistic Curriculum, 139-141):

★ The teacher should tell their students that co-operative learning is a priority and encourage sharing of materials and the development of communication skills. Smith claims that teachers often downplay co-operation. For example, he (1987) says: "I heard one teacher tell a class that has just completed a co-operative brainstorming session, "Okay, let's get back to work." The implication was that group work is entertaining but that real work begins when the students return to individual activities at their own desks." (p. 664)
★ The teacher should introduce the skills (e.g. listening, brainstorming) required for co-operative learning one at a time. Follow-up lessons on these skills should be introduced as necessary.

Structuring the following roles on learning teams promotes group success:

★ **Encourager of participation**: in a friendly way encourages all members of the group to participate in the discussion, sharing their ideas and feelings

★ **Praiser**: compliments group members who do their assigned work and contribute to the learning of the group
★ **Summarizer**: restates the ideas and feelings expressed in the discussion whenever it is appropriate
★ **Checker**: makes sure everyone has completed the assigned task and that everyone understands the general principles of the task (Glasser, 1986, p. 100)

Other roles may include:
★ **Timer**: ensures that the assigned tasks are being completed according to the schedule provided; manages use of time, etc.
★ **Presenter**: presents the groups findings/discussion/product to the class
★ **Reader**: reads the material/passage to the group
★ **Recorder**: takes notes on the groups discussion; acts as secretary; makes copies of notes for others; writes out presentation notes on chart paper, etc.
★ **Volume Control Person**: ensures that people are communicating at an appropriate level of volume and not disturbing others

Feedback may be provided to the group and within the group. Checklists of important social skills may be helpful to students. Teach students how to provide specific feedback, as it is the most constructive. The teacher needs to make social skills a priority in this process and not let them take a back seat to academic work. The two must be combined to promote optimum student intellectual, emotional and social growth.

Possible Activities (adapted from Miller, The Holistic Curriculum, 141):
★ Writing a skit/creating a performance piece; producing and performing it for class/community/cable TV
★ Discussing a book with a view to presenting conclusions/insights
★ Doing a research project
★ Creating a newspaper
★ Language study: (i.e. groups of three to study vocabulary); strong/average/weak student; groupings are based on a pre-test; each member looks up words independently and then they come together to discuss the meanings of the words they have looked up. After discussing the words, the students take two quizzes; one is a group quiz that the team works on co-operatively, the second is an individual quiz since Smith feels individual accountability is also important.

Visualization

Visualization is another strategy that is effective with all students, but particularly STARs. This strategy helps students focus and connect with their inner selves (although you may not want to identify it as such!). It may be used in the form of guided imageries (by a teacher or another student) or simple self-directed visualizations. Visualizations promote interdisciplinary connections in that poetry and imagery can be used to describe scientific concepts. They are also an effective way of personalizing the curriculum.

Visualization as a teaching strategy is multifaceted because it can be used to promote students' well being, students' performance on tests, and students' further understanding of the curriculum at hand. The following ideas (from M. Murdock's Spinning Inward) may be used as a starting point for incorporating visualization into the learning process:

★ Relax students before a test.
★ Have students visualize a part of a story as if they were living it. This visualization has been successfully used in English (e.g., a day in the life of Holden Caulfield) and in History (e.g., participating in the War of 1812).
★ In geography take students on a tour of the landscape.
★ In science or health, have visualize being a cell or take students through the water cycle.
★ Encourage students to experience the future by imagining how something will be. This is a good activity for career planning as well as taking on the perspectives of others in our society (e.g., the elderly). It is also an excellent way to develop self-concept as they can be asked to see themselves in ten years as a mother/father/person with a successful career, etc.
★ In goal setting, have students visualize themselves achieving a goal. Emphasize the feelings that accompany the achievement (e.g. rehearse a job interview).
★ Use a similar process in problem solving by having students visualize each step before taking it. This will promote more positive interactions with others where there has been a conflict and give students a sense of control over the outcome.
★ Have students visualize their ideal self. Emphasize the accompanying feelings and other peoples' reactions.

- ★ In order to develop skills, have students mentally rehearse doing a skill and doing it well. This techniques works in facilitating improved performances in any skill area. However, it is important that the student has an awareness of how the skill is performed correctly.
- ★ In order to enhance interpersonal skills, have students visualize themselves handling a potential conflict with another person smoothly and in control.
- ★ In order to enhance creativity, have students visualize an experience provided by the teacher (e.g., going underwater). Follow up with writing prose or poetry, journal writing, story telling or visual art.
- ★ In order to promote self-awareness amongst students try:
- ★ having students focus on a feeling that a certain event or character evokes. Students should let the image come to mind (give it time). It may take the form of a picture, a symbol, a colour or a word or feeling.
- ★ Have students turn that image into a metaphor and relate it to their life. What is the message of the metaphor? Dialogue with the image.
- ★ Foster the creation of the "ally within" by having students visualize behaving with a positive attitude in selected situations. Specific attitudes could include love, compassion or joy.

Journals

Journal writing is an activity that can be used in a number of ways for personal and academic purposes. In general, it is the act of reflection and/or chronicling through writing. The very nature of journaling makes it an effective strategy for use in all classrooms, especially those with students at-risk.

However, when it comes to classroom uses of journaling, there are a number of misconceptions and problems that may arise which may prevent it from being as useful or authentic an activity as it could be. The following is a list of benefits, issues and strategies which will maximize the use of journaling in the classroom for all students.

Benefits
Journals enable teachers to:

- ★ find out what has touched students
- ★ find out what students have learned
- ★ find out how the topic at hand connects to students' lives
- ★ make connections to the curriculum

★ make connections in their own lives
★ make connections with their teachers
★ make connections with the outside world

Journals enable students to:

★ write in a less inhibited manner
★ brainstorm ideas
★ practice the process of writing
★ understand the process of writing
★ see the connection between writing and thought
★ communicate knowledge of themselves
★ communicate knowledge of content
★ confront difficulties in their learning
★ organize their thoughts
★ make connections to previous experiences
★ reflect on other's perspectives
★ confront issues in their lives

Journals promote:

★ meaning-making
★ good thinking skills
★ metacognitive skills
★ reflection
★ creativity
★ dialogue between the student and the teacher
★ sharing of ideas
★ cross-curricular connections
★ problem-solving skills
★ interpersonal connections
★ reinforcement of learning on a personal level
★ different styles of expression
★ nourishment of the imagination

Forms
Journaling may take on the following forms, or a combination thereof:

★ Reflective (may take on a personal or curricular focus)
★ Stream of consciousness (to encourage creativity and brainstorming)
★ Metacognitive (to make connections)
★ Reader-response (e.g., take on a character's perspective)
★ Dialogue (between student and teacher/peer/self)
★ Learning diary (an account of how a student learns i.e., the problems they are having in math; what they thought of the last short story or unit, etc.)

Making the Most of Journaling in the Classroom
In order to make the most of journaling in the classroom, consider the
following strategies:

★ Make the purpose and possible audience of journals clear ahead of
  time so that students can feel safe writing them
★ Remember that in some cultures reflection/journaling is not as
  accepted or practised
★ Consider using peer responses rather than teacher responses (this also
  reduces the marking load)
★ Never mark journals for spelling and grammar; they are meant to be a
  free form of writing
★ Never judge (evaluate) journals; they are always correct
★ If you feel that you have to validate journals by marking them, try
  having the students develop/select the criteria on which they want to
  be evaluated
★ Try using simple stickers or checkmarks when students do not want a
  response
★ Journal with students to demonstrate their validity and model them
★ Try sharing your journals (be selective if they are) with the class
  (either as a group or one-on-one on a rotational basis)
★ Focus on quality not quantity
★ When students complain about journaling or ask how much they have
  to write, consider the topics you are using
★ In order to generate more interesting topics, have each student list ten
  topics which are of interest to them and use them randomly throughout
  the year; this makes students feel they are involved in the class and
  encourages them to look for their own topics
★ Use hypothetical questions ("What If…?") with fun and far-fetched
  scenarios (e.g. What would you do if you won a million dollars?)
★ Ask parents to respond to students' journals where appropriate
★ Consider having students discuss an issue/topic with a peer before
  writing their ideas down
★ In order to deal with the issue of repetition and redundancy in student
  writing, consider using visualization techniques or prompts prior to
  writing
★ Try using journals to expand students' awareness of different
  perspectives (i.e., ask them to take on the perspective of another
  person, a character or an object)
★ In order to reduce students' anxiety about sharing personal issues,
  employ a policy whereby students only hand in selected journals (i.e.
  one per week)
★ If students or parents do not see the value of journals, outline some of
  the benefits listed above, as well as any curricular connections

★ Rather than using journals solely as a response method, have students write on topics which pre-empt the next day's lesson; this will engage them more the next day

★ Establish confidentiality guidelines with students and outline the procedures involved with disclosures up front so that students disclosures may be taken as a sign that intervention is necessary

How to Respond

One of the biggest challenges of using journals in a classroom is knowing how to respond appropriately. The following guidelines may be useful in promoting effective teacher responses as well as student ease:

★ If students think you are reading their journals then read them
★ Do not hold onto journals for too long; students are anxious to read your response
★ Be non-judgemental
★ Do not trivialize the details and events of student journals
★ Accept what students have to say as valid and worthy of mention
★ Be positive
★ Use the opportunity to share your own related experiences or emotions
★ Ask questions
★ Only respond when students want you to
★ Try creating a checklist which students may submit with their journals indicating whether they want you to comment, dialogue with them, or not to respond at all

Dealing with Disclosure

For many students, school is a safe haven. Therefore, disclosures may be their only way of reaching out for help and trusting that the teacher will respond to them appropriately. Occasionally, a student will use journal writing to share personal information which is of a sensitive nature or poses a threat to others. If a student discloses information in their journal which suggests they are in a dangerous situation, please consult the **guidelines** in **Reaching for the STARs Part I** and share the information with a Guidance Counsellor/Administrator.

Format

Journals may take on a number of formats. In fact, they can include paragraphs, point-form notes, mindmaps, lists, quotes, questions, charts, phrases, key words pictures, symbols, etc. Encourage students to express themselves in the way that suits them best. If you have reluctant writers, try using the **Journal Writing Template on page 117** to structure and elicit a response.

Using Journals to Assess What Students Have Learned

Using journals to assess what students have learned can be far more effective than standard pencil and paper tests. Furthermore, they can be used across the curriculum. Reflective journals reveal the nuances and processes of the individual learning experience. Try using some of the following stems for prompting student reflection:

* ★ Last night I worked on...
* ★ I had difficulty with...
* ★ I experienced success with...
* ★ Everything was going great until...
* ★ I need to work on...
* ★ I can't seem to get my head around_____ because...
* ★ I don't understand...
* ★ What we learned today applies to my life because...
* ★ What we learned to day applies to the future because...
* ★ Why does...

Reflective journals can also be structured so that students may explain what they have learned in a meaningful context. One of the best tests as to whether someone understands something is to ask them to explain it in their own words or to teach it to someone else. The following questions are examples of how you can assess whether a student comprehends a concept:

* ★ How would you explain a fraction to your little brother?
* ★ How could you use the concept of fractions to divide up a pizza at your cousin's birthday party?
* ★ How does the concept of _____ relate to _____?

Journal Writing Template

Name:_____

_____

_____

_____

_____

_____

_____

_____

How does this topic relate to your life and experience?

_____

_____

_____

_____

_____

_____

What conclusions and reflections would you like to share?

_____

_____

_____

_____

_____

Chapter 7   Assessment and Evaluation for STARs

Assessment and evaluation have traditionally been seen largely as an administrative function of teaching. For many teachers, the goal of assessment and evaluation is to calculate a mark. Rather than being an end in itself, assessment and evaluation needs to be seen as part of a decision-making or problem-solving process where the focus is on factors in the environment such as pace, level, and presentation of learning material, rather than on identifying and labelling the student's deficits. (Stanovich, 49) Adaptive instruction responds by seeing assessment and evaluation as a means of designing interventions.

Traditional assessment and evaluation practices can overlook or discourage student success. For most students at-risk the assessment and evaluation process has been a large contributor to their negative experience in education. Rather than fostering their learning, it tends to foster their belief that they lack control over their performance and that they are incompetent. The student reacts by acting out or by becoming passive in the learning process. The inability of STARs to use traditional assessment and evaluation practices to improve their learning requires that we examine new ways of measuring and encouraging student success. New approaches to assessment emphasize the use of performances in real-life contexts (i.e., authentic performance tasks) that put skills and concepts in a meaningful context for the student. Students at-risk will benefit from this movement away from traditional paper and pencil tests.

Paradoxically, the ministry (with EQAO testing) has designed a measurement tool that is traditional in nature and is not designed to promote learning. Schools will be inclined to teach to the format and content of the test. Below are a number of strategies that promote a positive assessment and evaluation culture in classrooms with STARs, which contribute to long-term learning and better performance on the Grade Ten Test of Reading and Writing.

Administering Provincial Tests to Students At-Risk

Socio-Cultural Issues

While schools scramble to prepare for the Grade Ten Test of Reading and Writing, it is important to look at the big picture and remember the limited value and relevance of the test as a teaching instrument. And while EQAO is making an effort to create the best standardized test possible for Ontario, it is still a standardized test. The test is a direct reflection of the curriculum and will, in many cases, be biased against students who have limited exposure to the type of content contained and to the experiences presented within the test. The test is not a solution to these challenges but a yardstick by which to measure the gaps between our curriculum and our student populations. At this point there is no indication that test results will be used to meet these students' needs. *For further discussion of socio-cultural issues of assessment and evaluation, please see the section on Literacy page 51.*

Accountability Issues

"The distinction…between assessment and accountability is an important one to remember here. Accountability for all students does not mean that all students should participate in the same assessment program. What is important is that the ongoing progress and ultimate success of all students are consistently being accounted for." (Erickson, 7) Standardized tests are useful in that they enable us to assess how students are performing and what he/she needs to learn. Achieving a balance between professional accountability and sensitivity to individual needs is the challenge ahead of us.

Because of the sense of importance schools and society place on these tests, poor results may compound negative attitudes toward school and future performance in general. Sensitivity must be used in the classroom and in the community during standardized testing. Parents' councils may be useful in this effort. In general, students should be encouraged as much as possible to write the test. Schools must be clear as to what their motives are in excluding certain students or groups of students from writing the test. In fact, the very reasons that educators give for excluding students at-risk from standardized tests may reveal an attitude that inhibits the progress of STARs, in general. *(The following has been adapted from Elliott, 21-23.)*

1. **The test is too hard**: Educators and parents must ask why the test is too hard. If it is the format of the test then students must be retaught test-taking skills. If it is the content of the test, then one must ask what has inhibited the student from internalizing what has been taught in the Grade nine curriculum. Schools need to respond to these questions in new and innovative ways.

2. **Students are learning a different curriculum**: Why is that so? Is the student to graduate like the rest of the students? If so, then they should have the same standards and goals as other students.

3. **Students need accommodations which are not allowed on the test**: Accommodations should be provided in the regular instructional and assessment process in order to provide students with disabilities with equal footing. Similarly, all applicable accommodations outlined in the student's IEP should be provided for the standardized test. If these accommodations are not allowed, it is better to include students with accommodations than to exclude them and have no data at all.

4. **The student will become frustrated**: Test anxiety occurs for two main reasons:
   1. The student has not been taught or has not learned the content of the test.
   2. The student does not have adequate test-taking skills or is unfamiliar with the test format.

   Consider the following:
   1. What test accommodations does the student need to eliminate the effect of his/her disability?
   2. Has the student had sufficient opportunity to learn the content?
   3. Does the student have the necessary test-taking skills?

The following questions (adapted from *Testing Students with Disabilities*) may be helpful when determining the needs of individual students on standardized tests:

1. Can the student sit for the time expected?

2. Can the student complete the work in the time expected?

3. Can the student work quietly in a classroom setting for the time expected?

4. Can the student take the test in the same way that it is administered to other students?

5. Can the student work from a test booklet or do the pages need to be separated?

6. Does the student exhibit behaviours which are distracting to others?

7. Does the student take medication which may optimize the student's performance at a certain time of day?

8. Does the test need to be presented in a different manner (i.e., orally, with large print, with special equipment, etc.)

9. Does the order of presentation of the test (i.e. reading before writing) have the potential to affect student performance?

10. Does the student's IEP provide adequate accommodations to allow for optimum performance and if not, does it need to be revised in the regular classroom setting?

Standardized tests provide an opportunity to take a critical look at the needs of individual students. They also provide valuable insights into the way we perceive students with exceptionalities and how they are treated. Furthermore, school results need be put in a relevant and meaningful context if they are to be used effectively to foster school improvement.

The following guidelines may be helpful when administering provincial tests to STARs:

★ Postpone the writing of the test for students who are emotionally at-risk

★ Exempt students who are not pursuing an OSSD if they so choose

★ Postpone writing of the test if the student's performance may negatively impact on a positive trend of achievement

★ Involve students in the decision-making process and discuss the pros/cons of writing the test at this point in time

- ★ Consider whether the student has mastered the appropriate test-taking strategies
- ★ Consider whether the student has mastered the content being tested
- ★ Inform parents about the test dates/times and any lead-up activities the school is organizing
- ★ Discuss, openly and honestly, the issues surrounding inclusion and exclusion from standardized tests and how these decisions will affect future progress and interventions
- ★ Consult parents regarding decisions about postponements and exemptions
- ★ Remember that the test may be an effective tool for measuring strengths/weakness of test writing as well as reading and writing skills
- ★ Permit students to write the test in a one-on-one situation to alleviate anxiety (as outline in their IEP)
- ★ Provide scheduled breaks and relaxation techniques as necessary

For information on resources and timelines please contact EQAO's website at: www.eqao.org.

Learning Skills

Traditionally, students have been graded using a recognition of achievement, attitude, effort and behaviour. Students are often motivated to improve in these areas, responding to the philosophy that if the attitude and behaviour could be improved, the quality and quantity of work produced would also improve. This philosophy permits flexibility in programming for students at-risk. Currently, students are being evaluated on these Learning Skills separately. Making students aware of these skills and their importance in daily activities, as well as in the real world, will help students see their relevance in spite of the fact that they are no longer graded on them. The ministry has provided descriptors and rubrics for the Learning Skills. Teachers may want to try having students develop resumes and model letters of reference using the criteria outlined.

Group Marks

Traditionally, group work has been evaluated as a whole. This approach has permitted students with weaker academic skills to experience success and achieve higher grades. Currently, students must be awarded individual marks using the given academic criteria. One solution to this problem may be to assign tasks for each individual at the appropriate skill and content level.

Evaluating Using the "Most Recent and Consistent Level of Performance"

This philosophy of assessment and evaluation may benefit those students who "pull it together" at the last minute. However, it may be detrimental to those who have difficulty sustaining consistent levels of performance throughout the term, and especially at the end of the term. Teachers should use their best judgement to judge whether students have met the given expectations in a course. That is, marks of zero for missed assignments may be factored out of the student's mark if they have met those expectations in another assignment/activity.

Medians vs. Averages

In the past, teachers counted every assignment and factored them into the final grade using an averaging formula. Teachers are currently being encouraged to use a median formula and "eyeball" for a consistent mark. Using a median formula means that those marks which are the exception to the rule (i.e., the odd high mark) will not have the same affect as they did in the past in raising the average performance grade of the student. Teachers will need to carefully evaluate their methods of grading in order to assign fair grades.

Criterion-Referenced Standards

In the past, norm-referenced standards were used to assess a student's performance on any given task. Now, however, students must be evaluated according to the criteria set out in the given learning activity.

For example, can they effectively communicate their ideas orally? Teachers should consult the exemplars and rubrics provided by the ministry to refine this process.

Diagnostic, Formative and Summative Assessment

Diagnostic assessments should be used at the beginning of the course and each unit to assess which skills and concepts students have mastered and which need to be further developed before moving on. Students at-risk may have gaps in their learning which will need to be addressed. Using writing samples, discussion, observation as well as formal assessment tools will aid in the diagnostic process. Using visuals, demonstrations, dramatic exercises and real life contexts for learning will maximize what students do know and enable them to make connections in the classroom.

Formative Assessment is the mainstay of assessment and should be used on an ongoing basis to provide opportunities for students to master the required skills and concepts in a variety of contexts. Many STARs need more time and ongoing repetition to master new skills and concepts. Lessons should start with what students do know and scaffold from there. In addition, the teacher should provide students with a variety of contexts for learning a given set of skills/concepts and many opportunities for success **(see page 132 for chart)**. Assessing students in this manner promotes the greatest learning as it provides time for in-depth study and mastery. Formative assessment also permits students to achieve the highest-grade possible, as it is a measure of the most recent and consistent level of performance. According to current guidelines, formative evaluation can make up to 70% of the final grade. This design is conducive to students who tend to flounder on high-stakes evaluations or who avoid final evaluations.

Summative evaluation makes up 30% of the final grade and may be broken down in a number of ways. Oral presentations, videos, models, artistic representations, creative writing, interviews, performances and media products are just a few ideas. Summative evaluations should occur in a real life context where possible. Students are most likely to show their true level of mastery in this type of activity. This is also an indication that the evaluation has been designed well and is connected to student learning throughout the term; student grades should reflect their most consistent level of performance (**see page 133 for chart**). Teachers may want to provide students with choices as to the weighting of final evaluations in order to promote their strengths and their self-esteem. In some cases it may be appropriate for students to design final activities and rubrics. Such practices promote a sense of responsibility and involvement in the learning process and work towards dissolving negative attitudes towards the evaluation process.

Achievement Charts and the Overall Expectations

The Achievement Charts provide a flexible framework in which to assess students who are at-risk. Furthermore, plugging the Overall Expectations into this framework allows you to cover the general focus of the course without weighing you down with the assessment and evaluation of each and every Specific Expectation (**see 135-137 for examples from the Locally Developed English**). This flexibility is conducive to meeting the individual needs of students in the assessment and evaluation process and allows the teacher to evaluate holistically and equitably.

Exemplars

Providing clear expectations and criteria for evaluation promotes student success. Perhaps the clearest way of demonstrating what level of performance you want your students to work towards is by using exemplars. Exemplars allow students to see what is expected and to model their work on a preconceived standard; otherwise, this is often a difficult task on their own. Make an effort to collect past examples of desired products and make them available to students as they create their own. Furthermore, providing an array of products that range in quality is a good way to teach students to assess and grade the very work they will be doing. Allowing them to categorize each exemplar and match it to the rubric, or have them develop the rubrics based on the exemplars. Creating a clear set of criteria for evaluation will foster a sense of commitment and responsibility as students learn to understand the steps involved in achieving success as well as the desired level of quality.

Self/Peer Evaluation

Self evaluation can be used to foster a sense of accountability and responsibility for learning. The more students are involved in creating the criteria for evaluation and the more choice that is provided, the more they will 'buy into it'. The more connected students feel to the curriculum, the more effective and relevant it will be.

Similarly, peer evaluation can be highly effective when students feel connected to and supported by each other. Evaluation should be presented as part of the learning process and peers should be seen as fellow teachers. Peer evaluation works best when STARs are encouraged to show off an area of skill or expertise and share it with the class. One idea is to put individual students in charge of evaluating a given set of criteria, based on their area of strength. This opportunity will give students insight into the evaluation process and boost their self-esteems.

Rubrics

Rubrics are a great method of involving students in and scaffolding the learning process. When it comes to using rubrics, some care must be taken with students who are at-risk. While these assessment tools are always useful for teachers, they may be too text-heavy and abstract for students. Checklists are an equally effective and more accessible means of fostering clear communication and student success. However, if you decide to use rubrics, try designing them as a class. Introduce the concept of rubrics by having the class develop a rubric for "The Best Summer Vacation Ever" by listing the degrees of excellence across the chart. Please refer to the **Rubric for Laughs on page 134** for a mock rubric. This is a great way to introduce the concept into your classroom.

The following framework may be useful for designing rubrics with the class:

Purpose: What is expected is a quality piece of work.
Definition: We will know it is a quality piece of work because:
Strategies: To do a quality ____, it is necessary to:

Another strategy is to have students highlight the boxes in the rubric that indicate their current performance level as well as their desired level of achievement. This strategy helps students set short-term goals and makes rubrics more user-friendly.

To create an overview of the course, create a rubric using the Overall Expectations outlined in the curriculum document. A model has been created for you on **pages 135-137 for a Locally Developed English course (ENG 14M).**

Authentic Assessment

Assessment and evaluation are effective ways to **measure student progress, judge the need for instructional intervention** and **improve student learning**. In cases where these three criteria are not being met, the assessment and evaluation process is putting students further at-risk.

Authentic assessment provides opportunities for students to demonstrate what they know, can do, and are like. Authentic assessment moves away from paper and pencil tasks and explores real life issues which are relevant to students and to the real world. Such tasks develop academic skills as well as social skills (especially between students and the community). Authentic performance tasks put learning in a more meaningful context and help students develop their strengths.

Teachers need to be aware of their assessment practices and need to ask themselves what it is they are measuring when they use traditional methods. For example, are they interested in seeing how well a student can write an essay under pressure and time constraints or are they interested in measuring student knowledge or thinking skills on a given topic? Similarly, a mathematics test with many word problems will be unfair to students with weak language skills who have actually mastered the math problem-solving skills being tested. Educators need to ensure that students are demonstrating what they have learned and not how well they can take a test. Assessments that measure and reward incremental improvements are useful in motivating STARs. **See page 132 for the Checklist: Ensuring a Variety of Assessment Tasks** to track and plan a variety of assessments.

Communicating Results

Traditional tests are perhaps the most superficial and least effective tool for measuring student success. Furthermore, the grading system used tends to highlight errors and convey incompetence. When working with STARs, each and every assessment tool used should provide information about how students think and what they <u>do</u> know. The following guidelines may be helpful for communicating results to students at-risk:

★ results should be communicated in a positive manner
★ steps for improvement should be constructive
★ learning goals should be short-term and attainable
★ in order to give students a sense of accomplishment, they should be given the opportunity to work towards mastery of the given activity (not hurried on to the next one)

Assessment and Evaluation Strategies for Students At-Risk

1. Provide individualized incentive and reward structures that value student progress.
2. Help students develop specific, short-term goals that are challenging but realistic.
3. Distribute certificates and other awards on semi-regular intervals.
4. Encourage self-assessment to create awareness of the learning process.
5. Encourage peer assessment to foster a sense of community and support.
6. Test only what students have learned.
7. Provide fair and objective tests without any tricky wording.
8. Limit tests.
9. Use shorter, more authentic assessments.
10. Use a variety of evaluation techniques (written/oral/visual/performance, etc.) **(see page 76-77** for chart).
11. Structure learning and assessment into smaller units of study.
12. Provide structured, step-by-step learning/assessment of that learning.
13. Allow students to complete assignments in a way that promotes their success.
14. Provide choices and input in the evaluation process.
15. Do not use spelling as a criterion on tests/assignments which do not build editing directly into the process.
16. Encourage the use of a spell check when spelling counts.
17. Include the completion of a review package in the test/exam mark to show students the link between the two (e.g. give them 10 marks toward the final mark if completed).
18. Check student work/progress daily.
19. Give specific and positive feedback.
20. Treat assessment and evaluation as the tale that wags the dog; when you design an activity you should have a clear idea of what students will be evaluated on.

On the following pages are some templates to aid you in the assessment and evaluation process.

Checklist: Ensuring a Variety of Assessment Tasks
This checklist may be used to ensure that you are including a variety of assessment and evaluation methods.

Student Achievement Summary for Grading Purposes
This chart is designed to help you evaluate in the most effective way possible by looking at the overall patterns in student performance.

Course Rubrics
This set of rubrics plugs the overall expectations from the course into the achievement chart and is designed to help you plan and evaluate a course (the samples given are from the Locally Developed English course **ENG 14M). See Page 135-137**.

Checklist: Ensuring a Variety of Assessment Tasks

Unit: _____

Course: _____

Date: _____

OVERALL EXPECTATION (optional):				
ASSESSMENT TASKS:	**ACHIEVEMENT AREAS:**			
	Knowledge & Understanding	Thinking & Inquiry	Communication	Application
e.g., Quiz on Terms	X			
Journal			X	
Case study		X		

Student Achievement Summary for Grading Purposes

STUDENT:_____   **COURSE:**_____

STRAND: ——— OVERALL EXPECTATION:	Assessment Task						Highest, Most Consistent Level of Achievement	Positive Comments

Rubrics for Laughs

(/30)

CRITERIA FOR SUCCESS	Needs Improvement	Level 1 (50-59%)	Level 2 (60-69%)	Level 3 (70-79%)	Level 4 (80-100%)
COMPLETES QUALITY	Cannot recognize a building at all	Crashes into buildings when attempting to jump over them	Can leap over short buildings	Must take running start to leap over tall buildings	Leaps tall buildings in a single bound
	2	3	4	5	6
MEETS DEADLINES	Wounds self with bullet when attempting to shoot	Is a slow bullet	Not quite as fast as a speeding bullet	Is as fast as a speeding bullet	Is faster than a speeding bullet
	2	3	4	5	6
TAKES INITIATIVE	Smells like the bull	Shoots the bull	Is stronger than the bull	Is stronger than a bull elephant	Is stronger than a locomotive
	2	3	4	5	6
IS ADAPTABLE TO NEW SITUATIONS	Passes water in emergencies	Drinks water	Washes with water	Walks on water in emergencies	Walks on water without getting wet
	2	3	4	5	6
COMMUNICATES WELL	Loses arguments with self	Argues with him/herself	Talks to him/herself	Talks with angels	Talks with god
	2	3	4	5	6

KNOWLEDGE AND UNDERSTANDING (Course Rubric: Overall Expectations) LOCALLY DEVELOPED ENGLISH (ENG 14M)				
EXPEC-TATION	LEVEL 1 (50-59%)	LEVEL 2 (60-69%)	LEVEL 3 (70-79%)	LEVEL 4 (80-100%)
LRV.02	-demonstrates limited understanding of the elements of key literary and informational forms, with an emphasis on the features of textbooks, newspaper articles, short narratives, plays, and business letters	-demonstrates some understanding of the elements of key literary and informational forms, with an emphasis on the features of textbooks, newspaper articles, short narratives, plays, and business letters	-demonstrates considerable understanding of the elements of key literary and informational forms, with an emphasis on the features of textbooks, newspaper articles, short narratives, plays, and business letters	-demonstrates a thorough and insightful understanding of the elements of key literary and informational forms, with an emphasis on the features of textbooks, newspaper articles, short narratives, plays, and business letters
LRV.03	-demonstrates limited ability to identify and explain the effect of specific elements of style in informational texts	-demonstrates some ability to identify and explain the effect of specific elements of style in informational texts	-demonstrates considerable ability to identify and explain the effect of specific elements of style in informational texts	-demonstrates a high degree of ability to identify and explain the effect of specific elements of style in informational texts
MEV.01	-demonstrates limited ability to identify and describe the elements, intended audiences, and production practices of media forms	-demonstrates some ability to identify and describe the elements, intended audiences, and production practices of media forms	-demonstrates considerable ability to identify and describe the elements, intended audiences, and production practices of a variety of media forms	-demonstrates a high degree of ability to identify and describe the elements, intended audiences, and production practices of a variety of media forms

THINKING AND INQUIRY (Course Rubric: Overall Expectations)

LOCALLY DEVELOPED ENGLISH (ENG 14M)

EXPECTA-TION	LEVEL 1 (50-59%)	LEVEL 2 (60-69%)	LEVEL 3 (70-79%)	LEVEL 4 (80-100%)
LRV.01	-demonstrates limited ability to select, read, and demonstrate an understanding of a variety of literary and informational texts which are both personally meaningful and relevant to courses of study	-demonstrates some ability to select, read, and demonstrate an understanding of a variety of literary and informational texts which are both personally meaningful and relevant to courses of study	-demonstrates considerable ability to select, read, and demonstrate an understanding of a variety of literary and informational texts which are both personally meaningful and relevant to courses of study	-demonstrates a high degree of ability to select, read, and demonstrate an understanding of a variety of literary and informational texts which are both personally meaningful and relevant to courses of study
WRV.01	-demonstrates limited ability to use specific strategies to gather information and to generate ideas for written work	-demonstrates some ability to use specific strategies to gather information and to generate ideas for written work	-demonstrates considerable ability to use specific strategies to gather information and to generate ideas for written work	-demonstrates a high degree of ability to use specific strategies to gather information and to generate ideas for written work

COMMUNICATION (Course Rubric: Overall Expectations)

LOCALLY DEVELOPED ENGLISH (ENG 14M)

EXPECTA-TION	LEVEL 1 (50-59%)	LEVEL 2 (60-69%)	LEVEL 3 (70-79%)	LEVEL 4 (80-100%)
LAV.01	-demonstrates limited ability to use vocabulary and language conventions to read, write, and speak clearly and correctly	-demonstrates some ability to use vocabulary and language conventions to read, write, and speak clearly and correctly	-demonstrates considerable ability to use vocabulary and language conventions to read, write, and speak clearly and correctly	-demonstrates a high degree of ability to use vocabulary and language conventions to read, write, and speak clearly and correctly
LAV.02	-demonstrates limited ability to use listening techniques and oral communication skills to participate in large and small group discussions for a variety of purposes	-demonstrates some ability to use listening techniques and oral communication skills to participate in large and small group discussions for a variety of purposes	-demonstrates considerable ability to use listening techniques and oral communication skills to participate in large and small group discussions for a variety of purposes	-demonstrates a high degree of ability to use listening techniques and oral communication skills to participate in large and small group discussions for a variety of purposes

EXPECTA-TION	LEVEL 1 (50-59%)	LEVEL 2 (60-69%)	LEVEL 3 (70-79%)	LEVEL 4 (80-100%)
WRV.02	-demonstrates limited ability to select and use different literary and informational forms (e.g., procedures / instructions, explanations, supported opinions, reports, short anecdotal narratives, letters, Career Plan, AEP) for different audiences and different purposes	-demonstrates some ability to select and use different literary and informational forms (e.g., procedures / instructions, explanations, supported opinions, reports, short anecdotal narratives, letters, Career Plan, AEP) for different audiences and different purposes	-demonstrates considerable ability to select and use different literary and informational forms (e.g., procedures / instructions, explanations, supported opinions, reports, short anecdotal narratives, letters, Career Plan, AEP) for different audiences and different purposes	-demonstrates a high degree of ability to select and use different literary and informational forms (e.g., procedures / instructions, explanations, supported opinions, reports, short anecdotal narratives, letters, Career Plan, AEP) for different audiences and different purposes
WRV.03	-demonstrates limited ability to use an organizational pattern to structure ideas for writing texts	-demonstrates some ability to use an organizational pattern to structure ideas for writing texts	-demonstrates considerable ability to use an organizational pattern to structure ideas for writing texts	-demonstrates a high degree of ability to use an organizational pattern to structure ideas for writing texts
WRV.04	-demonstrates limited ability to use strategies for revising work	-demonstrates some ability to use strategies for revising work	-demonstrates considerable ability to use strategies for revising work	-demonstrates a high degree of ability to use strategies for revising work
WRV.05	-demonstrates limited ability to use strategies for editing and proofreading written work, with an emphasis on the conventions of Standard Canadian English	-demonstrates some ability to use strategies for editing and proofreading written work, with an emphasis on the conventions of Standard Canadian English	-demonstrates considerable ability to use strategies for editing and proofreading written work, with an emphasis on the conventions of Standard Canadian English	-demonstrates a high degree of ability to use strategies for editing and proofreading written work, with an emphasis on the conventions of Standard Canadian English
MEV.02	-demonstrates limited ability to use knowledge of media forms, purposes, and audiences to create media works	-demonstrates some ability to use knowledge of media forms, purposes, and audiences to create media works	-demonstrates considerable ability to use knowledge of a variety of media forms, purposes, and audiences to create media works	-demonstrates a high degree of ability to use knowledge of a variety of media forms, purposes, and audiences to create media works

Chapter 8   Incorporating Technology with STARs

Creating an Effective Program

> *"Maintaining access to technology throughout the student's school career, integrating technology so that it is available for all kinds of learning, and deploying uses of technology that move away from traditional teaching and learning methods are necessary components of a successful technology strategy for educating students at risk."* (Rossi)

Benefits

★ Having access to a computer makes students feel valued, especially when they do not have access to one at home

★ The physical presence of a computer helps students focus on the task at hand and concentrate for longer periods of time

★ Word processing helps develop student writing because: students can write for write longer periods of time; it enables them to reorder their ideas; it relieves the burden of handwriting for students who have difficulty; it promotes editing as part of the process of writing

★ Computers promote real-world applications of the curriculum

★ Using computers helps students develop their organizational skills

★ Using technology provides the opportunity for co-operative learning as students research projects and create presentations together

★ Using technology provides students the opportunity to share their knowledge of technology and to teach their peers

★ Using computer software promotes the development of problem-solving skills

★ Activities may be used to reinforce mathematical concepts through constructing spreadsheets and graphing the data.

★ Independent programs on computers (e.g. Pathways) provide the opportunity for self-pacing of programs and immediate feedback

★ Students are better able to create high-quality products (i.e., through editing)

★ It fosters computer literacy for potential employment opportunities

★ Computer stations in a classroom can open up opportunities for the teacher to interact one-on-one with students

★ Distance education opportunities on-line (e.g. The Eden Project) meet the needs of students in transition

Implementation

★ Investigate availability of technology in your school
★ Investigate various software programs; ensure there is a balance of drill-oriented and problem-solving oriented software available and that it is suitable to your students' needs and academic levels
★ Decide on how technology will be incorporated into the program
★ Develop a code of conduct
★ Establish a predictable schedule so that students will know when they have access

Curriculum Ideas

Desktop Publishing:	Create a class newspaper or magazine
	Resumes
	Letter writing
	Editing; peer editing
Applications	Databases
	Design software
	Graphing software
	Spreadsheets
	Graphic design
Web-based Activities:	E-mail etiquette and execution
	International correspondence
	Pen pals (within/outside of the school)
	Evaluating a website
	Creating your own/class website
	On-line research
	Media studies

Notes of Caution

★ Teachers should be careful that they choose software programs which are applicable to the curriculum
★ Teachers should be careful to ensure that chosen software programs are, in fact, addressing higher thinking skills and are not just drill activities.
★ Teachers should be aware of the limitations of technology as a tool; nothing can replace the importance of the student-teacher relationship
★ Teachers may want to disable some of the options so that students remain on task and make good use of their time
★ Teachers may need to limit the amount of time students spend on how things look and get them to focus more on the substance of their product

★ Teachers must ensure that computer technology is shared equitably across classrooms and within classrooms; structured schedules work best

Software

Each year software is purchased by the Ontario Software Acquisition Program Advisory Committee (OSAPAC) on behalf of all publicly funded schools. Consult www.osapac.org for a listing of available software.

The following section has been provided by Rene Aston Computer Resource Teacher YRDSB; Executive Director of SigElem (Special Interest Group Elementary)of ECOO Other Links

Meeting Expectations for Language and Mathematics

By far, the most widely used software meets expectations in language and mathematics. There are some programs that target the learning of skills.

Perfect Copy is an older type of program but nevertheless it is very useful to enhance editing skills. In addition, the program tracks student accomplishments. The student is presented with a short article in which there are many corrections to be edited. The student can select among many different types of areas to practice from commas to punctuation to confusing words to subject - verb agreement and more. The reading level extends from grade 4 to grade 8. The first articles are grade 4 level and the last articles are grade 8 level. Once all of the corrections have been made the students is notified of a perfect copy. The help feature can be modified to provide the student with more or less assistance. This program has been useful with students who exhibit written language difficulties and ESL students. The text can be printed and used for reading instruction as well. The articles are not identified as being for certain grade levels so that students are comfortable with selecting suitable passages for the level of language at which they function. There is even a utility for the teacher to enter text and set up exercises, however this procedure is time consuming. The time spent may be worthwhile as the teacher is able to support students in other subject areas such as science, geography or history during language class.

Math Trek 7,8,9 and Math Trek 10, 11, 12 are programs that focus on mathematical skills. Both programs were designed to meet the old curriculum outcomes, but they are still useful as many expectations in mathematics are similar to the previous curriculum. The student can access lessons, practise exercises and tests. Math Trek 7,8,9 covers Algebra, Fractions, Geometry, Graphing, Integers & Percent, Whole Numbers & Decimals, while Math Trek 10,11,12 covers Factoring, Systems of Equations, Coordinate Geometry,

Transformational Geometry, Statistics, Probability, Quadratic Functions and Second Degree Relations. There is a detailed student tracking system that reports on test results, averages and time on task. A calculator tool is available at the 7,8,9 level and a spreadsheet, charting tool, calculator, word processor with mathematical functions, algebra tiles and a probability tool are available with the 10, 11,12 level. Some of the lessons include animation and interactivity. This different method of presentation of concepts appeals to students and often reinforces the skills encountered in class and in the textbook. For students who require review in more basic mathematical skills there is Math Trek 4,5,6. This program has been recently developed and follows the ministry expectations closely while covering all 5 strands of mathematics.. All of the features of the two older programs are available in MathTrek 4,5,6. There are a variety of other mathematical software to reinforce skills including Mathville (mathematics set in daily life activities), Virtual Tiles, Zap A Graph and Geometer's Sketch Pad. Some of the software companies provide incentive packages for families to purchase software for use at home. Use the OSAPAC web site to located the software distributor's name and then contact the company for information on purchasing the software for home use.

Programs that can be used as tools for completing assignments include a variety of integrated packages that include a word processor, spreadsheet and database. One of the most intriguing recently acquired tool is Corel Presentations. Students are able to use this package to make web pages and slide shows to present information on many different topics. This tool is relatively easy to use, provides practice in industry standard software and can produce some spectacular results. Often these factors motivate students to aspire to try their best in completing assignments. Many programs have been licensed for teachers to take home for educational purposes, to learn the programs and to prepare assignments. Check the OSAPAC web site for the exact details.

Other Subject Areas

In other subject areas there are many useful programs for research purposes including the Ultimate Human Body, the Digital Rain Forest, and ArcView GIS, to name a few. Just recently acquired is Simply Accounting for business courses or life skills training. Note that one of the requirements of OSAPAC is that the software is available in English and in French. Many software programs fulfil that requirement.

Career Cruising and Career Explorer (web service included) provide another avenue of research for Teacher Advisory Programs. With this software and service, student will acquire up to date information on careers, as well as a variety of career planning tools.

Software Availability for the Future

Every year in the spring, OSAPAC sets priorities for software acquisition. Teachers across Ontario are invited to voice their opinions by completing a survey on the OSAPAC web site. This year (summer 2000), the priorities are the following:

1. Career Education - Grades 9-12. To support the career education component of the Choices into Action Program and the Career Education course.

2. Language - Writing Grades 4 - 10. To support remediation at many grade levels leading up to the Grade 10 Language Test, OSAPAC is looking for software to support language writing improvement.

3. Atlas for Grades 4 - 10. An up-to-date, web supported multi-media atlas is needed to support many areas of the new curriculum including history and geography, Canadian and World Studies, Social Studies and Science.

4. French Science software for Grades 4 - 8.

5. Graphic Organizer for Grades 4 - 12. There are over 30 references to Graphic Organizers in the new curriculum and many more references to "organizers". The ability to graphically represent ideas easily and dynamically will be of use across the curriculum.

6. Graphic Editor for Grades 4 - 12. There have been requests over the last two years for OSAPAC to license a Graphic Editor product. This is now mentioned frequently in the high school curriculum. The Graphic Editor products provide a range of image manipulation possibilities from the basic up to high level animation and 3-D graphics." (OSAPAC web site)

Teachers can look forward to several new programs to assist them in meeting ministry expectations. Check the web site (www.osapac.org) for an update on the availability of programs.

Professional Development Opportunities

With the wide variety of software available, the focus of implementation shifts from locating the appropriate resources to professional development. Many boards provide courses in specific software applications. ECOO Educational Computing Organization of Ontario) runs a conference in May as well as providing a journal 4 times a year for educators in Ontario. Check out more information about this organization at www.ecoo.org. Subject associations are now embracing the use of technology and are sources for information. On the OSAPAC web site there is a listing of resources for teachers. Select "Software" and then "Ontario Curriculum Links" from the OSAPAC home page www.osapac.org. Another organization, ENOREO (Educational Network of Ontario) provides a forum for discussion on many topics related to education, projects for students and links to information. Visit their web site at www.enoreo.on.ca. Seventeen course profiles for grade 10 developed on the Curriculum Planner can be downloaded from Media-x web site at http://planner.media-x.com/download. The federal government supports a national site for educators called SchoolNet at www.schoolnet.ca. In addition many boards provide links for teachers on their own board web sites.

Chapter 9   Evaluating Your School: School Surveys

Stop – Start -- Continue

Try using the following framework at department and staff meetings to reflect on past practices and create future goals and dreams. The idea is to list all of the things one would like to see start, stop, and continue regarding a certain practice or policy. This will enable schools to pool and incorporate the input of staff in a constructive and efficient manner.

Stop – Start—Continue Input Form

Topic: _____

Please provide input on the given topic using the following framework:

STOP

START

CONTINUE

Adaptive Instructional Practices Survey

Use the following checklist *(Adapted from <u>Integrated Education</u>)* to assess whether you incorporate adaptive instructional methods to meet the needs of STARs.

Effective Instructional Planning

- ❑ set clear goals; these should be specific, short-term, and based on your monitoring of individual students
- ❑ set high expectations for each student (not just the class)
- ❑ demand high success rates
- ❑ check for student understanding
- ❑ provide direct and frequent student feedback
- ❑ design co-operative learning opportunities

Effective Instructional Management

- ❑ establish and post classroom rules and procedures, and explicitly communicate expectations about classroom behaviour
- ❑ position yourself to be able to monitor the total class and scan the classroom frequently
- ❑ develop a sense of co-operation, accountability and responsibility in students
- ❑ develop a co-operative rather than a competitive learning structure
- ❑ contact and collaborate with parents
- ❑ by good planning and management, maximize the amount of time you give to instruction

Effective Instructional Delivery

- ❑ assign tasks that are relevant to instructional goals
- ❑ identify each student's level of skill and knowledge development and build on it
- ❑ match tasks to student level
- ❑ persist in constructing understanding when it needs developing
- ❑ use demonstration, concrete examples, prompts and practice to convey ideas and concepts
- ❑ model thinking skills (metacognitive skills – make the obvious obvious)
- ❑ teach learning strategies (study/test-taking/reading strategies, etc.)
- ❑ ask questions and prompt for responses
- ❑ ask questions that require more than a yes-no answer
- ❑ sequence or scaffold your questions
- ❑ ask what-where-why-when-how questions
- ❑ reword questions when student fails to respond or is incorrect
- ❑ get students actively engaged
- ❑ maximize student-teacher interaction about academic topics
- ❑ provide frequent feedback to students

Effective Monitoring and Evaluation

- ❑ check for student understanding (use why, what, and how questions)
- ❑ provide many opportunities for students to respond
- ❑ monitor actively and frequently
- ❑ evaluate what is taught (keep records, work samples, etc.)
- ❑ inform students of progress and set goals with them
- ❑ keep instructional objectives at hand and check for specific evidence that they are being achieved

Teacher Efficacy Survey (Adapted from "How Efficacious are You?")

Teachers are often affected in negative ways by the circumstances that pervade the teaching environment. As a result, it is very important that teachers are centred and focused on their own personal growth as a part of the teaching process. Beliefs and attitudes have a pronounced effect on teaching – and more importantly – on learning: "Beliefs influence teacher motivation and effort, teacher-student interactions, and student achievement." (DiBella-McCarthy, 68)

Points for Reflection and Discussion

How Well Do You Know Yourself as a Teacher?

★ Do you have high hopes and positive expectations for your students, or are you discouraged by their performance?
★ Do you take credit for their successes and their failures?
★ Do you blame them for their lack of progress or make excuses for them?

Complete the survey on page 154 and reflect on how beliefs affect your teaching and the learning of your students. When you are finished, use the following interpretations to reflect on your practices and your teaching well-being.

★ If you scored 25 or higher in Column A you have a high sense of teaching efficacy and you take responsibility for the success of each student in your class.

★ If you scored above 20 in Column B, you probably have low personal teaching efficacy. The following suggestions will help you reach your ideals:
  1 Identify and adapt your skills to meet student needs.
  2 Provide more direct instruction to groups of students and maintain high rates of student engagement throughout the lesson.
  3 Keep an eye out for trouble spots – be proactive in your assessment practices and make interventions before behaviours erupt?

★ If you scored 20 or higher in Column C, you believe that your ability to effect change is limited by external factors. The following suggestions may help you accomplish your sense of teaching efficacy:
1   Develop a positive mindset.
2   Believe in the potential of your students.
3   Establish realistic expectations for your students and yourself.
4   Actively seek support from home and school

★ If you scored above 25 in Column D, you probably have high personal teaching efficacy. You put forth the effort required to overcome barriers and feel confident in your ability to make a difference with your students.

Summary

The way that teachers see students has a powerful impact on learning. According to Anne Jordan (Integrated Education, 86-90), an expert on adaptive instruction, teachers can be categorized as restorative, preventive or in transition.

The **restorative teacher** sees the student as the source of the problem and believes that they are ill-equipped to deal with the specialized demands of the given exceptionality tend to avoid instructional interaction with the student; reasons for this may include a lack of confidence on the part of the teacher or a lack of responsibility for the learning of the child. (Jordan, 92)

The **preventive teacher** has a high level of efficacy and sees learning difficulties as a challenge that he/she shares with the student; he/she also seeks in-class support and expects assessment data to provide him/her with insight into the learning difficulty. (Jordan, 92)

According to this model, providing the collaborative support of a resource person whose role is to work with the teacher (in-class) rather than exclusively with the students is an ideal support for restorative teachers.

In order to identify your own attitudes, complete the **Checklists on page 152.**

For further exploration of this subject, please refer to *Making a Difference: Teachers' Sense of Efficacy and Student Achievement* (Ashton & Webb, 1986).

Self-Efficacy Quiz

Consider each statement below and indicate the extent to which you agree or disagree with it. There are four possible ratings:

(1) Strongly disagree   (2) Disagree   (3) Neutral   (4) Strongly agree

In the box next to the statement, please write the number that best describes your opinion or your self-perception.

Statement	A	B	C	D
I am confident in my abilities as a teacher				□
With the right techniques and materials, all students can learn.	□			
When a colleague boasts about student progress I feel inadequate		□		
New research in education is just "old wine in new bottles."			□	
Some students are beyond my reach.		□		
The socio-economic status of a student is not a critical variable of effective teaching.	□			
I am adept at behaviour management and handling discipline.				□
Even the worst home situations should not interfere with a teacher's ability to teach students.	□			
My enthusiasm for teaching makes me an effective teacher.				□
In a given class, students from low-income backgrounds will probably not do as well academically as students from middle or upper class homes.			□	
There is little I can do to prevent the failure of my low-achieving students.		□		
Students' disabilities are challenges, not obstacles, that motivate teachers to do a better job.	□			
I am making a difference in the lives of my students.				□
There is little I can do to influence change in a student from a dysfunctional or broken home.			□	
If students did not act out in class, I could do what I am trained to do – teach.		□		
Sometimes the out-of-school problems of students overwhelm teachers; it is no wonder teachers cannot teach.			□	
I have never met a student I could not teach.				□
A teacher is only one person; only a miracle can help some kids.			□	
If teachers provide a positive role model for students, even those experiencing negative influences at home can succeed.	□			
My students' progress is a reflection of my teaching.				□
Teachers have little effect on student motivation to learn.			□	
My students know that I care about them, and they try hard to meet my expectations.				□
Effective teachers are powerful influences in the lives of their students.	□			
Most of my colleagues seem to be more innovative and resourceful than I am.		□		
Powerful teaching can overcome many negative home environmental factors.	□			
There is little I can do to help a student who just doesn't care about learning.		□		
Good teachers continually search for new ideas for research and in-service training to enhance teaching.	□			
I am confident in my subject matter and can answer students' questions in depth.				□
A teacher's influence on student achievement is limited compared to the influence of the home environment.			□	
In some subjects I feel I am just a page or two ahead of my students.		□		
Certain disabilities of my students interfere with my ability to teach them.			□	
When my students fail to make the expected progress, I get discouraged and begin to doubt my skills as a teacher.		□		

Add up your responses in each column

	A	B	C	D
Total	□	□	□	□

TEACHING EXCEPTIONAL CHILDREN/Spring 1995

A Restorative Teacher:

★ Assumes the student has a condition that can be labelled, that is inherent, and that can't be modified much
★ Assumes that integrating the student is only done for social reasons
★ Requests an assessment to confirm the existence of the condition
★ Has not tried many prerefferal interventions to see what the student is able to do or what the student needs; he/she claims this will slow down the process of getting help for the student
★ Expects the child to be withdrawn once the condition is diagnosed
★ Assumes that resource-withdrawal will deal with the condition and do not attempt to link up the curriculum with the resource program
★ Reports to parents in isolation from the resource teacher

A Teacher in Transition:

★ Assumes the student's problem will respond to intervention, but gives up effort after three or four tries
★ Assumes that integration is morally right, but is afraid of how it will affect other students
★ Requests assessment to identify the problem "just in case"
★ Has accumulated information about the student's learning patterns but hasn't modified the program
★ Expects the resource teacher to take over now and solve the problem
★ Cooperates with the resource teacher but isn't prepared to share ownership of the problem
★ Involves the parent(s)/guardian(s), but hopes the resource teacher will lead the discussion

A Preventive Teacher:

★ Assumes that the student's problem is temporary and can be circumvented or solved in the classroom
★ Assumes that integrating the student will extend resources through the school day and allow the student the opportunity to succeed
★ Requests an assessment to identify learning style, gaps in skills, learning strengths, and needs
★ Tries prereferral interventions prior to requesting assessment and has accumulated much information about the student
★ Expects resources to be provided to the teacher in the classroom to assist in solving the problem
★ Assumes that the resource teacher will fit any programming into the teacher's classroom curriculum; withdrawal, if any, will be used to assist the student in the classroom
★ Involves parents from the outset and regards them as part of the problem-solving team

School Survey

★ The following survey is meant to create an overall picture of how well your school is supporting the needs of students at-risk and is designed to help you troubleshoot areas in need of improvement.

★ Please refer to relevant sections of the resource book to address areas of concern.)

★ Rate each of the following criteria on a scale of one to three, three being the highest score.

★ Compare the scores from each section to assess areas in need of development. Try to look for recurring themes and identify which groups are most in need. (Do not get overwhelmed by your list of needs. Taking initiative in one area tends to effect considerable change across the school.)

Assessment and Evaluation Practices

1 2 3   Assessment practices used complement the abilities of students.
1 2 3   Assessment practices contribute to the learning of all students.
1 2 3   Assessment is done on an ongoing basis.
1 2 3   A variety of assessment strategies are used across the curriculum.
1 2 3   Evaluation criteria are made explicit to students.
1 2 3   Students share responsibility of in the assessment and evaluation.
1 2 3   Learning skills are emphasized in the classroom.
1 2 3   Assessment practices are consistent across the curriculum.
Notes: (/24)

_____

_____

Behaviour

1 2 3   Student behaviour is dealt with in a proactive manner.
1 2 3   Positive behaviour is highlighted and rewarded.
1 2 3   Consequences for inappropriate behaviour are meaningful and relevant.
1 2 3   All staff are aware of the protocol for dealing with inappropriate student behaviour.
1 2 3   All staff are consistent in their expectations and in the application of consequences.
1 2 3   All staff are aware of the protocol for dealing with attendance concerns.
1 2 3   All students are aware of their rights and responsibilities in the school.
1 2 3   Students are given the opportunity to take on responsibilities in the school.
1 2 3   All staff are aware of the crisis intervention plan and the resources available to support staff and students in times of need.
Notes: (/27)

_____

_____

Community Involvement

1 2 3   The school has partnerships with community agencies and organizations which meet the needs of a broad spectrum of students.
1 2 3   The police have opportunities to interact with the school population in a positive manner.
1 2 3   Socio-cultural agencies and organizations are involved in meeting the needs of different socio-cultural groups in the school.

Notes: (/9)

_____

_____

Curriculum

1 2 3   The curriculum is stimulating to all students.
1 2 3   The curriculum is relevant to all students.
1 2 3   Authentic performance tasks are the main focus of curriculum design.
1 2 3   Teachers and departments are encouraged to employ integrated curriculum models.
1 2 3   The curriculum is presented in a socially relevant context.

Notes: (/18)

_____

_____

Environment

1 2 3   The school plant is welcoming and invitational.
1 2 3   Student art work is displayed throughout the school.
1 2 3   All students have a place to call their own.

Notes: (/9)

_____

_____

Instruction

1 2 3   All teaching staff are aware of the individual needs of exceptional students as outlined in their IEP.
1 2 3   Teachers across the curriculum contribute to the IEP.
1 2 3   All teaching staff are aware of the difference between accommodations and modifications.
1 2 3   Instruction focuses on meaningful learning activities instead of rote learning.

1 2 3   Homework assignments are meaningful and relevant.
1 2 3   Co-operative learning is one of the main strategies used.

Notes: (/18)

Literacy

1 2 3   The school has a cross-curricular literacy committee.
1 2 3   All teaching staff have an understanding of what literacy is and how it classrooms/subject areas.
1 2 3   Teachers have an understanding of the role that literacy plays in the families and lives of all members of the school community.
1 2 3   All teaching staff employ literacy strategies in their classrooms/subject areas.
1 2 3   The school has a cross-curricular literacy committee.

Notes: (/15)

Parent/Guardian Involvement and Support

1 2 3   Parent(s)/Guardian(s) are involved in meaningful dialogue on school issues.
1 2 3   Parent(s)/Guardian(s) are involved in strategic planning at each and every opportunity.
1 2 3   The Parent Council membership is representative of all of the socio-cultural groups in the school.
1 2 3   All communication to parent(s)/guardian(s) is clear, straightforward and uses simple language.
1 2 3   All open houses and parents' nights are accessible to all parents.
1 2 3   There are special supports in place for parent(s)/guardian(s) of students in ESL programming.
1 2 3   All staff are aware of the protocol and resources available for enlisting support for parents.
1 2 3   Transportation and childcare are provided whenever possible.
Notes: (/24)

Professional Climate

1 2 3   Current information and strategies are shared with all staff.
1 2 3   There are sufficient resources (e.g., technology and equipment) to do the job well.
1 2 3   All staff are involved in goal setting.
1 2 3   The implementation of new mandates and initiatives addresses the needs of all staff.
1 2 3   Professional development is offered on and ongoing basis and responds to the needs of staff.
1 2 3   School policies and procedures are defined and communicated.
1 2 3   All staff feel safe and valued.

Notes: (/21)

_____

_____

Programs

1 2 3   The school's mission statement reflects the needs of all students.
1 2 3   All staff are aware of the various pathways and destinations available for students to work toward the achievement of a diploma.
1 2 3   Locally Developed programs are in place or being applied for.
1 2 3   Programs are as heterogeneous in their student make-up as possible.
1 2 3   Co-curricular programs (social and academic) exist to meet the needs of students at-risk.
1 2 3   Work experience is an integral part of school programming.

Notes: (/18)

_____

_____

Student Involvement

1 2 3   Students play a positive and meaningful part in the school.
1 2 3   Students from across the population participate in co-curricular activities.
1 2 3   Positive relationships exist between students of different socio cultural groups in the school.
1 2 3   Peer support is enlisted and provided by and for all students for the purposes of academic and social support.
Notes: (/12)

_____

_____

Student Support

1 2 3   All staff are familiar with the protocol around reporting incidents where student welfare is at risk.
1 2 3   Proactive intervention strategies are in place to meet the needs of at-risk students.
1 2 3   Students and parents are involved in short-term and long-term goal setting.
1 2 3   Opportunities for peer mediation and mentoring exist as part of the school program.

Notes: (/12)

_____

_____

Support Staff

1 2 3   All staff are acquainted with the roles and qualifications of the various support staff in the school.
1 2 3   All support staff feel part of the school team.

Notes: (/6)

_____

_____

Teacher Support

1 2 3   All new teachers have received an orientation of the school, its policies and programs.
1 2 3   All new teachers have a mentor to consult with in times of need.
1 2 3   School committees are representative of the entire staff.
1 2 3   The school has a representative for teachers, department heads and support staff to speak on behalf of their needs and concerns.

Notes: (/12)

_____

_____

TOTAL: ___
                219

RESOURCES

Amoja Three Rivers'. Cultural Etiquette , 1990

Ashton, P. A., Webb, R.B. Making a Difference: Teachers' Sense of Efficacy and Student Achievement. New York: Longman, 1986.

Ballen, J. and Moles, O., *Strong Families, Strong Schools.* (U.S. Department of Education); http://ericweb.tc.columbia.edu/families/strong/index.html#sfhomepage (Visited July, 2000)

Baxter, Sheila. A Child is Not a Toy: Voices of Children in Poverty. Vancouver: New Star Books, 1993.

Beattie, M. "Connecting Mind, Heart, & Soul – An Exemplary Secondary School." *Orbit* (vol. 30, no. 2, 1999), p. 34-37.

Beatty, B. "Teacher Study/Support Groups – An Antidote to Burnout and Demoralization." *Orbit* (vol. 30, no. 2, 1999), p. 23-25.

Bicard, D.F., "Using Classroom Rules to Construct Behaviour.*" Middle School Journal.* Columbus, OH: May, 2000, p. 37-40.

Brackenbury, Cheryl.. Peer Helpers Plus, A comprehensive training manual to help student tutors and other facilitators make the grade. Pembroke Publishers Ltd., 1995.

Canfield, Jack & Wells, Harold. 100 Ways to Enhance Self-Concept in the Classroom, Chicken Soup for the Teenage Soul. Health Communications, Inc.Deerfield Beach, FLA, 1995

Colorose, Barbara. The Discipline Game: Winning at Teaching. Educational Consulting Associates: Onglewood, Col., 1982

Costello, Catherine; Palmer, Ted; Smitheram, Mary Lou. Contacts: Teaching Literacy and Communication across the Curriculum. Toronto: OSSTF, 1997.

DiBella-McCarthy, H., McDaniel, E. A., Miller, R. "How Efficacious Are You?" Teaching Exceptional Children, 1995, 68-72

Drake, S.M., "A Novel Approach to Integrated Curriculum – The Story Model." *Orbit*. (vol. 23, no. 2 Collector's Edition – Holistic Education in Practice, p. 5-7).

Dropping Out: The Cost to Canada, Conference Board of Canada, 1992. http://www.tlp.on.ca/cyf/History&Rationale.html

Eisner, J. *The London Free Press*. (July 14, 2000) Knight Rider News Service. http://specialedition.net/cgi/se4...

Elliott, J., Ysseldyke, J., Thurlow, M., Erickson, R. "What About Assessment And Accountability? – Practical Implications for Educators." *Teaching Exceptional Children*, Sept/Oct, 1998, 20-26.

Englert, C., Tarrant, K., Mariage, T. "Defining and Redefining Instructional Practice in Special Education: Perspectives on Good Teaching." *Teacher Education and Special Education*. 1992, vol. 15, no. 2, 62-86.

Eric Reports, p. 37) Fax 703 440 1408 U.S. Department of Education ED 334 510 published in 90 61 p

Erickson, R., Ysseldyke, J., Thurlow, M., Elliott, J. "Inclusive Assessments and Accountability Systems - Tools of the trade in Educational Reform" *Teaching Exceptional Children*. Nov/Dec 1998, 4-9.

Fischer, C. "An effective (and affordable) intervention model for at-risk high school readers." *Journal of Adolescent & Adult Literacy* (43:4 December 1999/January 2000)

Foster, Elizabeth Sabrinsky. Tutoring: Learning by Helping. A student handbook for training peer and cross age tutors. Revised Edition. 1992.

Gordon, K. "Managing Your Classroom." North York Schools

Hackworth, M., Eckman, A. "Conflict Resolution" *The Toronto Star*. Toronto: Knight Rider Productions, Inc., 1999.

Handbook for Teachers. Prentice Hall: Englewood Cliff, N.J., 1976

Impact 2000 - Report of Impact of Government Reform on Education. OSSTF (AMPA) March, 2000

Jordan, A., Lindsay, L., Stanovich, P. J. Abstract: "Classroom Teachers' Instructional Interactions with Students Who Are Exceptional, At Risk, and Typically Achieving." *Remedial and Special Education*. Vol. 18, No. 2, March/April 1997, p. 82-93.

Jordan, A. Skills in Collaborative Classroom Instruction. London: Routledge, 1994.

King, A. J. C. and Coles, B. J. The Health of Canada's youth: Views and behaviours of 11, 13, and 15 year-olds from 11 countries. Ottawa: Health and Welfare Canada.

Lazare, Gerald; Nicholls, Sherry; Shallhorn, Jack. Mindscapes: Teaching for Multiple Intelligences. Toronto: OSSTF, 1997.

"Long Awaited Legislation – the Duty to Report Abuse." OSSTF Update, Vol. 26 #17: http:/www.osstf.on.ca/www/pub/update/vol26/1ju/1jualeg.html) (Visited July, 2000)

Melaville, A. *Together We Can: A Guide for Crafting a Profamily System of Education and Human Services.* Providing Effective Schooling for Students at Risk (U.S. Department of Education and U.S. Department of Health and Human Services, 1993)1996: North Central Regional Educational Laboratory. http://ericweb.tc.columbia.edu/families/strong/index.html#sfhomepage

Miller, J. The Holistic Curriculum. Toronto: OISE Press, 1996.

Miller, J. The Holistic Teacher. Toronto: OISE Press, 1993.

Miller, J. "Presence and Soul and the Classroom." *Orbit* (vol. 30, no. 2, 1999), p. 10-11.

Moles, O., ed. Reaching all Families: Creating Family-Friendly Schools" Pennsylvania Office of Education Research and Development, Aug. 1996. *http://eric-web.tc.columbia.edu/families/strong/index.html#sfhomepage)* (Visited July, 2000)

Murdock, M. Spinning Inward. Boston: Shambala, 1987.

Nagel, G. The Tao of Teaching - The Ageless Wisdom of Taoism and the Art of Teaching. *(New York: Penguin Putnam Inc., 1994)*

Noyes, H. Clarke, Phd.. "The Goose Story". *ARC NEWS*, Vol. 7 NO. 1, January, 1992.

Peers Empowering Peers (P.E.P.). A senior led program for Grade 9s. Lifecycle Counselling, 1999. email: lifecycle@sympatico.ca See also: www.parent-watch.com

Positive Peer Solutions. One Answer for the Rejected Student Phi Delta KanDan) Oct 99

Postman, N. The End of Education – Redefining the Value of School. New York: Vintage Books, 1995.

Quinn, M. M., Osher, D., Warger, C. L., Hanley, T. V., Bader, B. D., Tate, R., Hoffman, C. C. 2000. *Educational Strategies for Children with Emotional and Behavioural Problems.* Washington, DC: Center for Effective Collaboration and Practice.

Report of the Royal Commission on Learning – Short Version, Ministry of Education. (1995) www.edu.gov.on.ca/eng/general/abcs/rcom/short/short.html (Visited July, 2000)

Reaching for the STARs................................161

Resources for Better Schools. The Advantage Press, P.O. box 3025, Lisle, Illinois. USA 60532.

Rogers, S. and Graham, S. The High Performance Toolbox. (Evergreen, CO: Peak Learning Systems, Inc.), 1998.

Rosenburg, Steven L., McKeon, Loren M., and Dinero, Thomas E. Positive Peer Solutions. One Answer for the Rejected. *Phi Delta Kappan*, vol. 81, Number 2. October, 1999.

Rossi, R.and Montgomery, A. eds., Education Reforms and Students at Risk: A Review of the Current State of the Art. (American Institutes for Research - U.S. Department of Education, January 1994); http://www.ed.gov/pubs/EdReformStudies/EdReforms/title.html (Visited July, 2000)

Rushowy, K., "Grade 9s play summer catchup.' Toronto Star. July, 12, 2000.

Stanovich, P., Jordan, A. Integrated Education. Toronto: Federation of Women Teacher's Associations of Ontario, 1995

The Stork is Dead: Straight Answers to Young People's Questions About Sex: Shedd C. WordBooks. Waco, Texas

Tobin, L. What Do You Do With A Child Like This – Inside the Lives of Troubled Children. Duluth, MN: Whole Person Associates, 1998.

Zucker, M.A., Judge. Lecture: Youth and the Courts. Partners in Management – Peterborough, Ontario: January 21, 1998.

Supplementary Readings

Anti-Racism

Antiracism Education – getting started. A practical guide for educators.
Toronto: OSSTF, Feb 2000.

Willinsky, John. Learning to Divide the World – Education at Empire's End.
Minnesota: The University of Minnesota Press, 1998.

Assessment and Evaluation

O'Connor, K. How to Grade for Learning. (Arlington Heights, IL: Skylight
Training and Publishing, Inc.). 1999.

Rolheiser, C. Self-Evaluation…Helping Students Get Better At It! Toronto:
The Clear Group, 1996.

Behaviour

Colorosa, Barbara. The Discipline Game: Winning at Teaching. Educational
Consulting Associates: Onglewood, Col., 1982

Emmer, Admund T., Evertson, Carolyn M., Sanford, Julie P, Clements, Barbara
S., Worsham, Murray E., Classroom Management for Secondary
Teachers. Allyn and Bacon, USA

Jones, Fredric H. Positive Classroom Discipline McGraw Hill USA 1987

Kohn, A. Punished by Rewards: The Trouble with Gold Stars, Incentive Plans,
A's, Praise, and other Bribes. Boston: Houghton Mifflin, 1993.

Best Practices

Best of Effective Practices. Progress Review of Ontario's New District School
Boards; Education Improvement Commission, 2000.
http://eic.edu.gov.on.ca

Classroom Strategies

Glasser, W. Control Theory in the Classroom. New York: Harper and Row,
1986.

McCarney, S. Prereferral Intervention Manual. Columbia, MO: Hawthorne,
1995.

Oppenheimer, Jo. Getting it Right: Meeting the Needs of the Early Adolescent
Learner. Toronto: Federation of Women's Teachers' Association of
Ontario, 1990.

Curriculum

Drake, S. Developing an Integrating Curriculum Using the Story Model. (Toronto: OISE Press, 1992).

Gardner, H. Frames of Mind: The Theory of Multiple Intelligences. New York: Basic Books, 1983.

Gardner, H. Multiple Intelligences: The Theory in Practice. New York: Basic Books, 1993.

Goldstein, Arnold P. The Prepare Curriculum Research Press, USA 1988

O'Sullivan, E. Transformative Learning. Toronto: U of T Press, 1999.

Family and Community Involvement

Marshak, D. The Common Vision: Educating and Parenting for Wholeness. New York: Peter Lang, 1997.

General

Hixson, J., Tinzmann, M.B.,. Who Are the "At-Risk" Students of the 1990s? NCREL, Oak Brook, 1990

Tobin, L. What Do You Do With A Child Like This – Inside the Lives of Troubled Children. Duluth, MN: Whole Person Associates, 1998.

Zvirin, Stephanie, The Best Years of Their Lives A Resource Guide for Teenagers in Crisis. American Library Association, 1992

Holistic

Flake, C. ed. Holistic Education: Principles, Perspectives and Practices. Brandon, VT: Holistic Education Press, 1993.

Glazer, S. (ed.) The Heart of Learning: Spirituality in Education. New York: Tarcher/Putman, 1999.

Goleman, D. Emotional Intelligence. New York: Bantam, 1995.

Holistic Education – A Framework for Curriculum. Waterloo Region Roman Catholic Separate School Board, 1992.

Jackson, P., Delehanty, H. Sacred Hoops – Spiritual Lessons of a Hardwood Warrior. New York: Hyperion, 1995.

Miller, John. The Contemplative Practitioner: Meditiation in Education and the Professions. Toronto: OISE Press, 1994

Miller, John. Education and the Soul: Toward a Spiritual Curriculum. Albany, NY: SUNY Press, 1999.

Palmer, P. To Know as We Are Known: A Spirituality of Education. San Francisco: Harper, 1983.

Peer Tutoring

Brackenbury, Cheryl. Peer Helpers Plus – A Comprehensive Training Manual to Help Student Tutors and other Facilitators Make the Grade Pembroke Publishers Limited, Markham, Ontario. 1995.

Foster, Elizabeth Sabrinsky. Tutoring: Learning by Helping – A Student

Handbook for Training Peer and Cross Age Tutors. Educational Media Corporation, Minnesota 1992.

Poverty

Baxter, Sheila. A Child is Not a Toy. New Star Books Limited, Vancouver, 1993.

Maeroff, Gene I. Altered Destinies – Making life Better For Schoolchildren in Need. 1998 Library of Congress Cataloging-in-Publication Data

Sexual Harrassment

Ball, K., Martyn, P. "Sexual Harrassment." *Education Forum*. Toronto: OSSTF, Spring, 1999.

Sexuality

Pride & Prejudice – working with lesbian, gay and bisexual youth. Edited by: Margaret S. Schneider, Ph.D. Central Toronto Youth Services, 1997

Social Issues 11 – A Guide to AIDS Substance Abuse Violence Eating Disorders OSSTF, 1990.

Socio-Cultural Issues

Brathwaite, K. S., James, C. E., eds. Educating African Canadians. Toronto: James Lorimer and Company Ltd., Publishers, 1996.

Delpit, L. Other People's Children: Cultural Conflict in the Classroom. New York: The New Press, 1995.

Dickar, M. "Teaching in Our Underwear: The Liabilities of Whiteness in th e Multi-Racial Classroom." University of Minnesota. http://www.lib.wmc.edu/pub/researcher/issueXi-2/dickar.html

Hopkins, R. Educating Black Males – Critical Lessons in Schooling, Community, and Power. New York: State University of New York Press, 1997.

McIntosh, P. "White Privilege: Unpacking the Invisible Knapsack," reprinted In *Independent School*, Winter 1990.

Willinsky, J. Learning to Divide the World – Education at Empire's End. Minneapolis: Regents of the University of Minnesota, 1998.

Teaching

Canfield, Jack & Wells, Harold. 100 Ways to Enhance Self-Concept in the Classroom,

Crealock, Carol, and Bachor, Dan G. Instructional Strategies for Students with Special Needs. Allyn & Bacan Canada, 1995.

Gordon, F. Noah. Magical Classroom – Creating Effective, Brain Friendly Environments for LearningU Zephyr Press, Arizona, 1995

Palmer, P. The Courage to Teach. San Francisco: Josey-Bass, 1998.

Posner, George J. Field Experience, A Guide to Reflective Teaching. New York: Longman, 1985

Violence

Garbarino, James, PH.D. Lost Boys – Why Our Sons Turn Violent – and How We Can Save Them. 1999, The Free Press

Women

"An Educator's Guide To Creating Safe Learning." Canadian Congress for Learning Opportunities for Women. Toronto: 1999 cclow@web.apc.org

ABILITY GROUPING (see: Streaming)

ADOLESCENT EXPERIENCE, April 1993

AIDS, March 1990

AIDS: SCHOOL POLICIES, March 1990

ALTERNATIVE EDUCATION, June 1991

APPRENTICESHIP AND INDUSTRIAL TRAINING PROGRAMS, April, 1996

CAREER EDUCATION, April 1996

CHANGE PROCESS IN EDUCATION, September 1999

CONFLICT RESOLUTION, June 1998

DISCIPLINE, October 1999

DROPOUTS, February 1993

EFFECTIVE SCHOOLS, June 1998

FULL SERVICE SCHOOL, February 1996

HOLISTIC CURRICULUM, September 1996

LITERACY, September 1997

MENTORING/INTERNSHIP, March 1992
(TEACHER TO TEACHER) (For students helping students, see: Peer Counselling/tutoring)

NATIVE EDUCATION, June 1992

PARENT COUNCILS (See: School Advisory Councils)

PARENT-TEACHER CONFERENCES, April 1982

PART-TIME EMPLOYMENT, STUDENT, April 1996

POVERTY AND EDUCATION, December 1999

RACE RELATIONS AND MULTICULTURALISM, May 1994

SCHOOL ADVISORY COUNCILS, March 1999

SCHOOL-COMMUNITY RELATIONS, April 1995

SCHOOL-TO-WORK, June 1995

SUICIDE, November 1995

THINKING SKILLS, October 1993

VIOLENCE AND VANDALISM, February 2000

VOLUNTEERS IN EDUCATION, February 1998

YOUNG OFFENDERS ACT, February 1992